Brancusi's Endless Column Ensemble

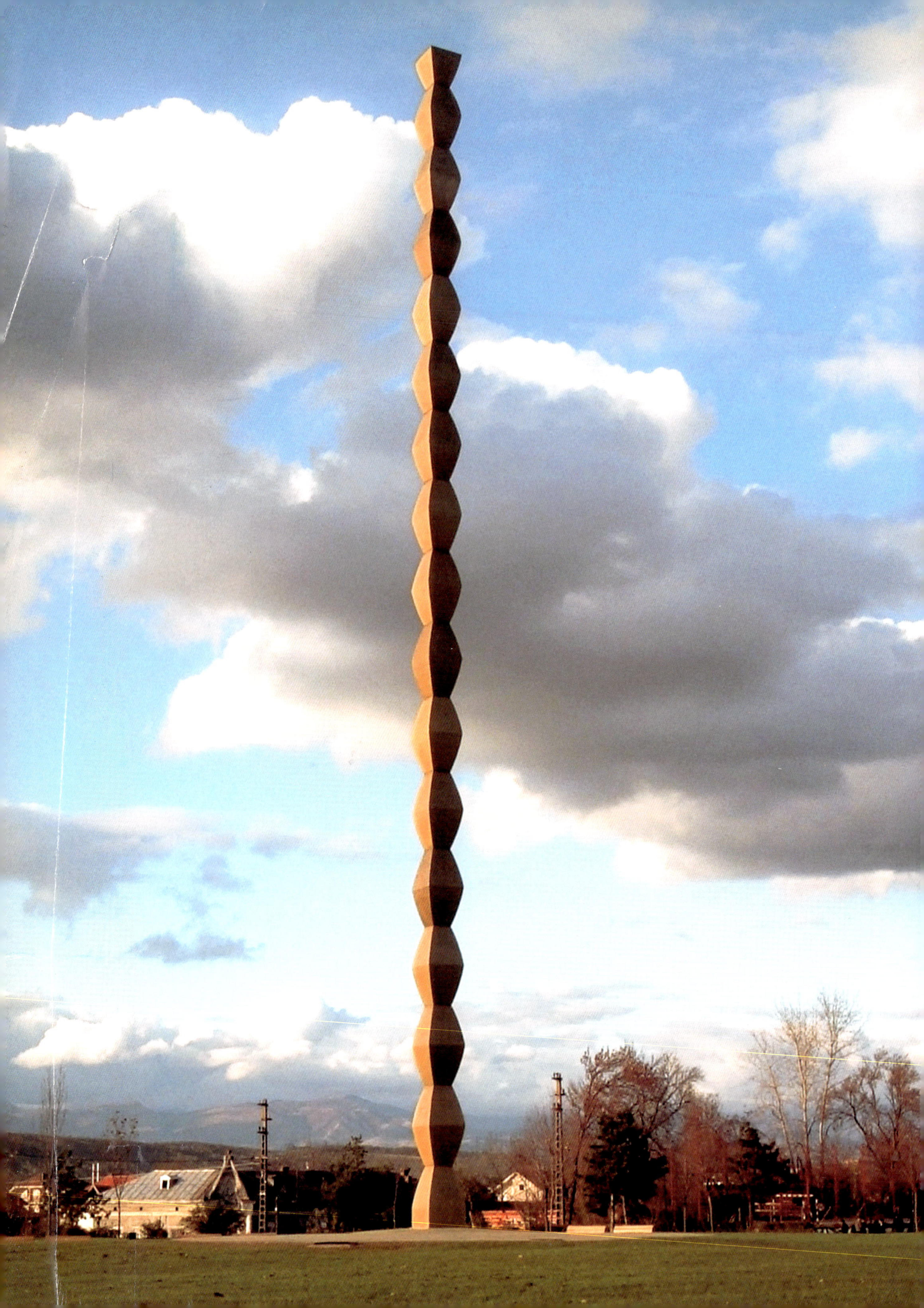

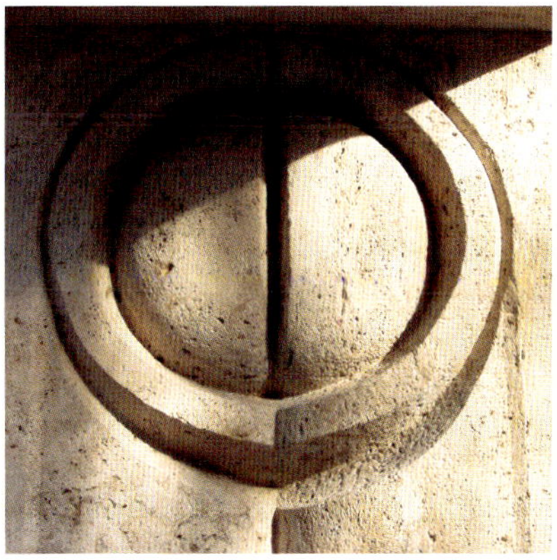

Brancusi's Endless Column Ensemble

Târgu Jiu, Romania

Essays by Sorana Georgescu-Gorjan,
Richard Newton, Alexandra Parigoris,
Mihai Radu and William Tucker

Edited by Ernest Beck

This volume is published to celebrate the completion of the restoration of Brancusi's sculptural ensemble

Support for this publication has been generously provided by:
The Beirne Foundation, Inc.
International Music and Art Foundation

WORLD MONUMENTS FUND

SCALA

Support for the entire publications programme of the World Monuments Fund has been provided by The Brown Foundation, Inc. of Houston, the Paul Mellon Estate and The Beirne Foundation, Inc.

First published in 2007 by
Scala Publishers Ltd
Northburgh House
10 Northburgh Street
London EC1V 0AT
UK

ISBN-13: 978-1-85759-436-2

Edited by Ernest Beck
World Monuments Fund Series Editor: Angela M. H. Schuster
Project Manager: Annabel Cary
Designer: Andrew Shoolbred
Printed and bound in China

10 9 8 7 6 5 4 3 2 1

All works are by Constantin Brancusi unless otherwise stated

All photographs are provided by the World Monuments Fund except as detailed in Photographic Credits (page 80)

Every effort has been made to acknowledge correct copyright of images where applicable. Any errors or omissions are unintentional and should be notified to the Publisher, who will arrange for corrections to appear in any reprints.

Frontispiece: The restored *Endless Column*, 1938, showing the Carpathian Mountains in the distance
Page 3: Detail from *Gate of the Kiss*, 1938

Contents

Foreword 6
Mica Ertegün

Introduction: WMF and the Endless Column Ensemble 8
Bonnie Burnham

PART I: CREATION OF THE ENDLESS COLUMN ENSEMBLE

Brancusi and his Return to Romania 12
Alexandra Parigoris

From Dream to Reality: Construction of the *Endless Column* 30
Sorana Georgescu-Gorjan

PART II: THE CHALLENGE OF TÂRGU JIU

Restoration of the *Endless Column*, *Table of Silence* and *Gate of the Kiss* 42
Mihai Radu

Reclaiming Sacred Space 54
Richard Newton

Urban Redevelopment and a Visionary New Visitor Centre 64
Mihai Radu

The Legacy of Târgu Jiu 70
William Tucker

Acknowledgements 78
Bibliography 79
Photographic Credits 80

Foreword

Mica Ertegün

I am delighted to witness the successful outcome of the World Monuments Fund's Watch® programme through its involvement in the restoration of Constantin Brancusi's monuments in Târgu Jiu. This venture was timely and renewed a historic association between Brancusi and the country that can justifiably claim to be one of the first to promote the artist's work outside his native Romania. The World Monuments Fund welcomed the opportunity to renew this support for the art of Brancusi, and in particular the monumental ensemble, which all regard as his most significant achievement.

Brancusi is acknowledged as the leading modernist sculptor of the first half of the twentieth century, but it is arguably the monuments at Târgu Jiu that ensure his reputation is passed on from generation to generation, each in turn finding new ways of understanding what his forms signify and the temporalities they explore.

I wish to thank all those involved in the restoration, in Romania and the USA, not forgetting scholars from the worldwide community who lent their support with perseverance and enthusiasm. The work could not have been completed without this remarkable team effort.

OPPOSITE View from the raised bank of the River Jiu down to the *Table of Silence*, 1938, following landscape restoration, 2006

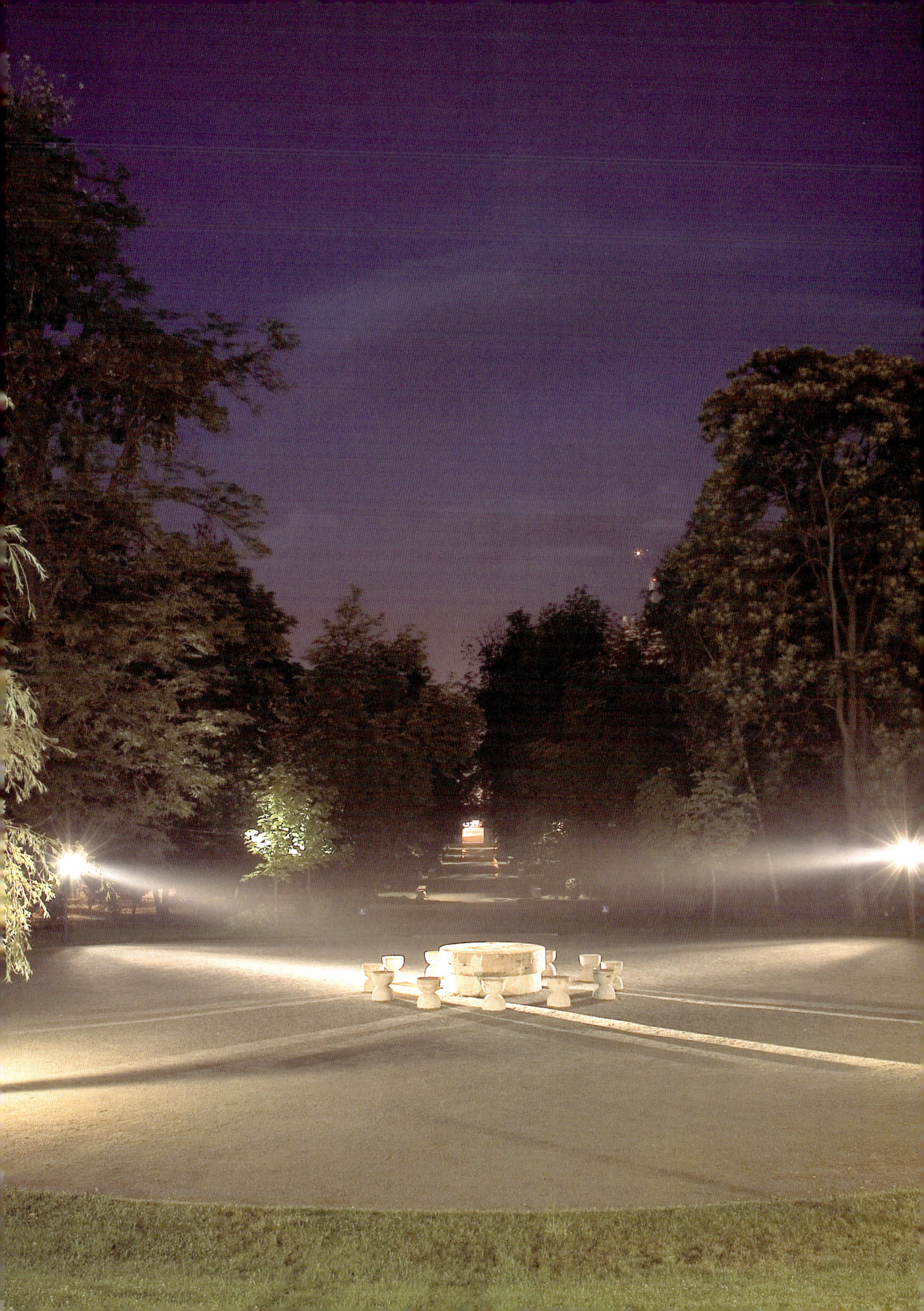

Introduction: WMF and the Endless Column Ensemble

Bonnie Burnham
President, World Monuments Fund

When the World Monuments Fund (WMF) launched its World Monuments Watch® programme in 1996, we could not have foreseen the wealth and range of important cultural sites around the world that were in an imperiled state. The biennial list of *100 Most Endangered Sites* has often had the effect of catapulting these sites into the public spotlight and unleashing a process, both political and cultural, which has proved critical to the restoration process. These special case histories become the success stories of the Watch® programme and help us to accomplish our mission of saving the world's most important imperiled landmarks.

Brancusi's legendary *Endless Column*, a pilgrimage destination for lovers of modern art, is one such case. Located in the remote small town of Târgu Jiu, in western Romania, it was in a state of severe neglect when it was nominated onto the Watch® list in 1995. Rumours suggested that the entire spine of the *Column* was compromised and it could collapse at any minute. The vertical string of modules of its outer form were darkened, with the bronze finish being completely absent in many areas, revealing an alarmingly rusty and pitted substrate.

The *Endless Column* appeared on our first Watch® list in 1996. Shortly thereafter I attended the launch of a cultural heritage financing initiative at the World Bank. I made the suggestion to a World Bank staff member that the *Endless Column* would make a worthy pilot project for the programme, since its restoration would be a catalyst to local development. I soon heard back from him that the Romanian government was very interested in the idea. WMF worked with the Romanian Ministry of Culture to develop a proposal for a $5 million financing programme of which the *Endless Column* restoration would be the centrepiece. WMF committed additional funding to permit the project to be conducted by the highest international standards. A partnership was launched, which has continued to evolve and, in the process, is inspiring local development and enhancing local appreciation of this great masterpiece.

OPPOSITE Section of the restored *Endless Column* (pre-landscape restoration), showing Avenue of the Heroes and Church of Apostles Peter and Paul in the background

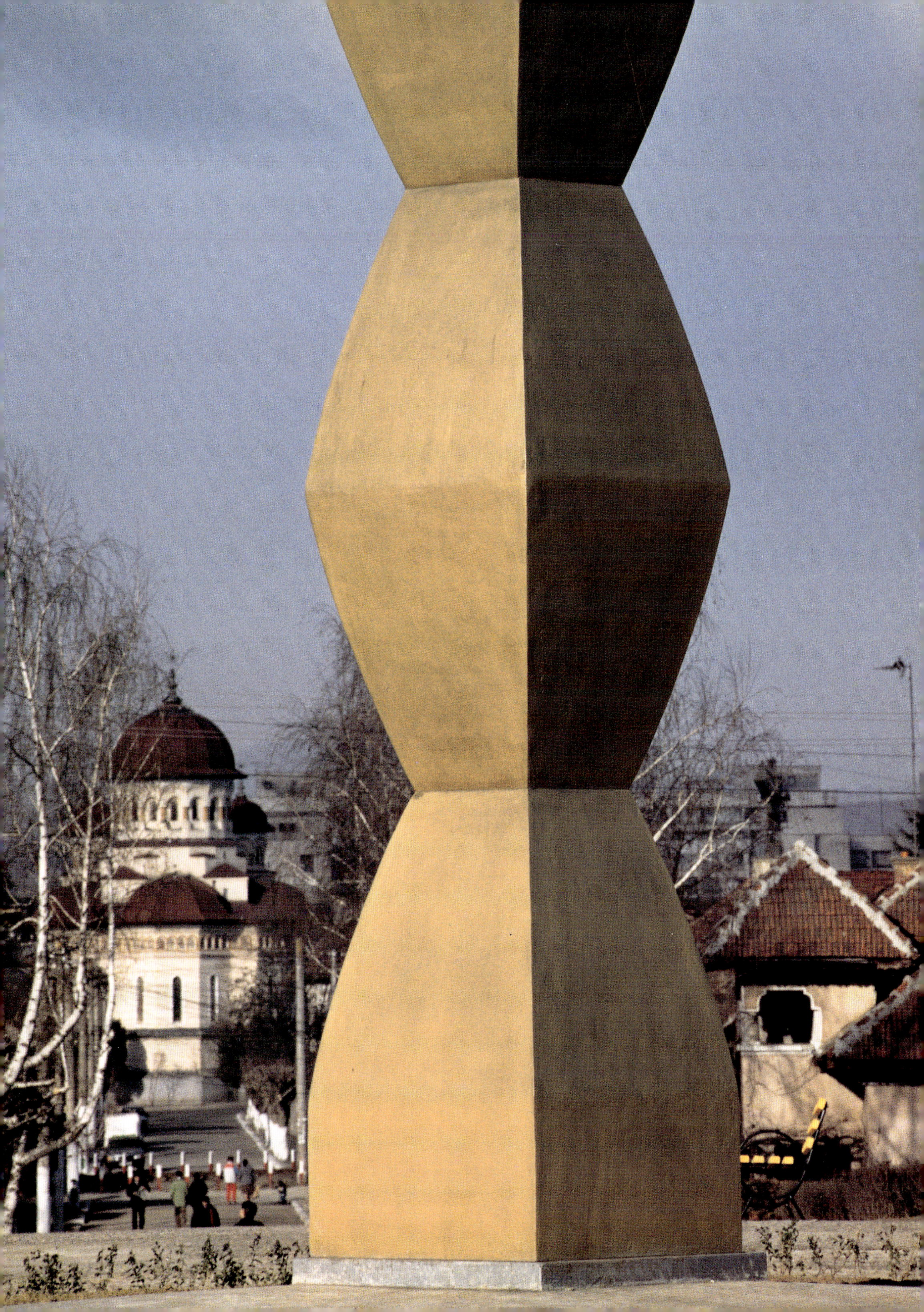

There were several controversial issues surrounding the restoration of this colossal work in metal: how to restore the surfaces of the modules to recreate the original finishes intended by the artist; whether to replace or retain the steel spine, the ingenious invention of Romanian engineer Stefan Georgescu-Gorjan; and how the monument should be presented to the public within a town, the urban fabric of which had been scarred in recent decades by Ceaucescu's urban demolition programme known as 'systemization'. WMF played a pivotal role in orchestrating a scientific consensus on these points, and in providing outstanding international experts to guide the process to completion. Romanian experts crafted the solutions based on the philosophy we developed through a series of workshops and expert visits.

The *Endless Column* is part of an ensemble designed by Brancusi to commemorate a key moment in Romanian history. The battle of Târgu Jiu, in

Detail of *Endless Column*, following its restoration in 2000

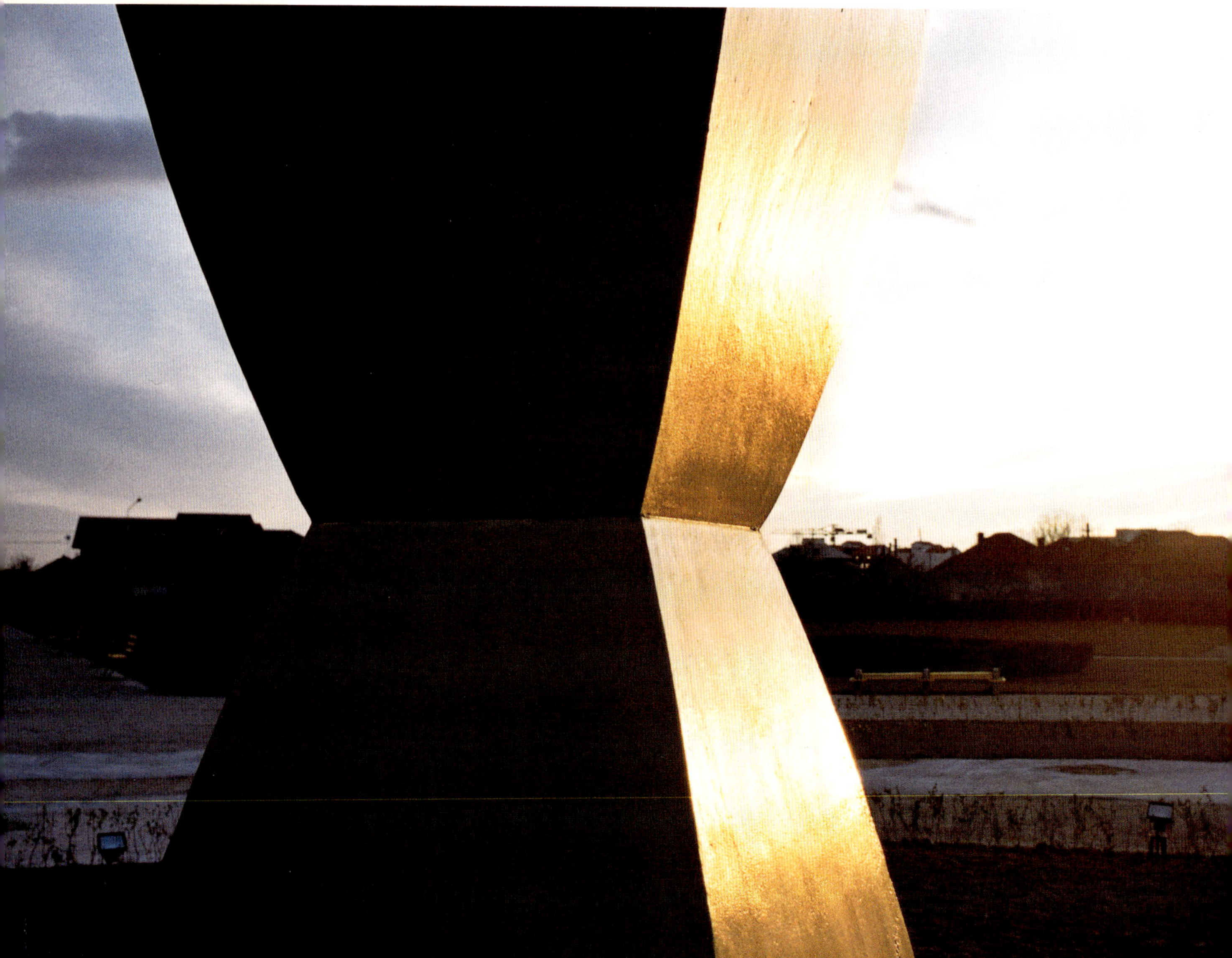

November 1916, was a triumph because it held off approaching German forces long enough to allow the Romanian army time to regroup; it was also a moment of tragic loss of young men who successfully defended the town. Brancusi created a tribute to this poignant victory by designing three monumental sculptures that occupy opposite ends of the town. The procession along the road that joins them – the 'Avenue of the Heroes' – takes the visitor through the heart of the town where these young men lived, to a place of high ground, surrounded by expansive sky, where the *Column* rises to the heavens. Deeply religious, Brancusi created an almost mystic experience of contemplation and inspiration.

Recapturing this experience was one of the necessary and challenging aspects of the project. In addition to cleaning the two stone sculptures included in the ensemble, WMF led the innovative re-landscaping of the sculpture parks, to create joyous but respectful surroundings, where the artworks can be appreciated and revered. Sad and neglected public spaces have been transformed into welcoming and compelling vistas.

More yet remains to transform Târgu Jiu back into the picturesque town it once was, to attract and welcome foreign visitors. WMF is now at work, in partnership with the Romanian-based Infinitului Foundation, to build a visitor centre near the *Endless Column*, where visitors can relax and contemplate the sculpture while learning about its restoration and its important place in the art of the twentieth century.

Several key individuals were the mainstays of WMF's ten-year effort to save the Endless Column Ensemble, by providing financial support as well as affirmation throughout the course of a long and complex undertaking. Today that effort is complete, and we can again enjoy the serene beauty of Brancusi's only monumental outdoor work. The results that have been achieved could scarcely have been imagined at the outset. Furthermore, hopefully, ten years from now, we will be able to look back and realize how much this project has done to revitalize the area, where visitors can enjoy the beauty of the country's landscape, the power of its history and the diverse, colourful customs of its people.

For 40 years WMF has been engaged in this process of transformation at many sites around the world, bringing together the financial and technical resources necessary to preserve these great works and to restore their pivotal role in the local environment. WMF acts as a catalyst, initiating a process that will grow through the efforts of local partners. Every project – like the present one – provides opportunities to expand our knowledge and our know-how, to engage many individuals in this process and to create a stronger public awareness of the important role great buildings play in all of our lives.

As we complete the extraordinary accomplishment that this restoration represents, we also salute our local partners – most especially the mayor of Târgu Jiu and the dedicated staff of the Ministry of Culture and the World Bank – who have worked beside us to create the consent and enthusiasm without which the project could not have happened.

Brancusi and his Return to Romania

Alexandra Parigoris

Born in 1876, in the small village of Hobitsa, not far from Târgu Jiu, in the Gorj region of Romania, Constantin Brancusi left his native land in 1904 and set off for Paris, where he chose to pursue his career and live for the rest of his life. In many respects, his decision to return to Romania, in 1937, to undertake the important commission for Târgu Jiu, follows a pattern of artistic careers that one often encounters throughout Europe during the nineteenth and twentieth centuries. A talented youth of humble origins is singled out by his contemporaries at an early stage; he gains access to schools providing training; and embarks on a journey that draws him into wider cultural circles and larger cities. Having built a reputation, he sometimes achieves success on an international level, as in the case of Brancusi, and only then returns home as a celebrated personality to produce a significant work of art.

Brancusi's career follows this simple narrative and puts in perspective the stories that have grown up around him, many of which he himself told and promoted. Still, the narrative fails to account adequately for the many factors that contributed to his fame and it certainly does not provide the viewer – who is encountering the extraordinary monuments at Târgu Jiu for the first time – any means of coming to terms with them. To gain a deeper understanding of what Brancusi created at Târgu Jiu, it is important to understand the impact that his education and subsequent career had on the development of his artistic sensibility.

OPPOSITE Brancusi's studio as reconstructed in 1977–90 in the Centre Pompidou, Paris. Detail showing three wooden versions of the *Endless Column* and the plaster prototype version for the *Endless Column* at Târgu Jiu

EDUCATION AND 'CIVILIZATION THAT SPOILS EVERYTHING'

At the end of the nineteenth century, Romania, like so many Eastern European nations, had only recently gained its autonomy, having emerged from the hegemony of the Ottoman Empire. The newly established monarchy with its German-born king, Carol I, and its democratically elected parliament were

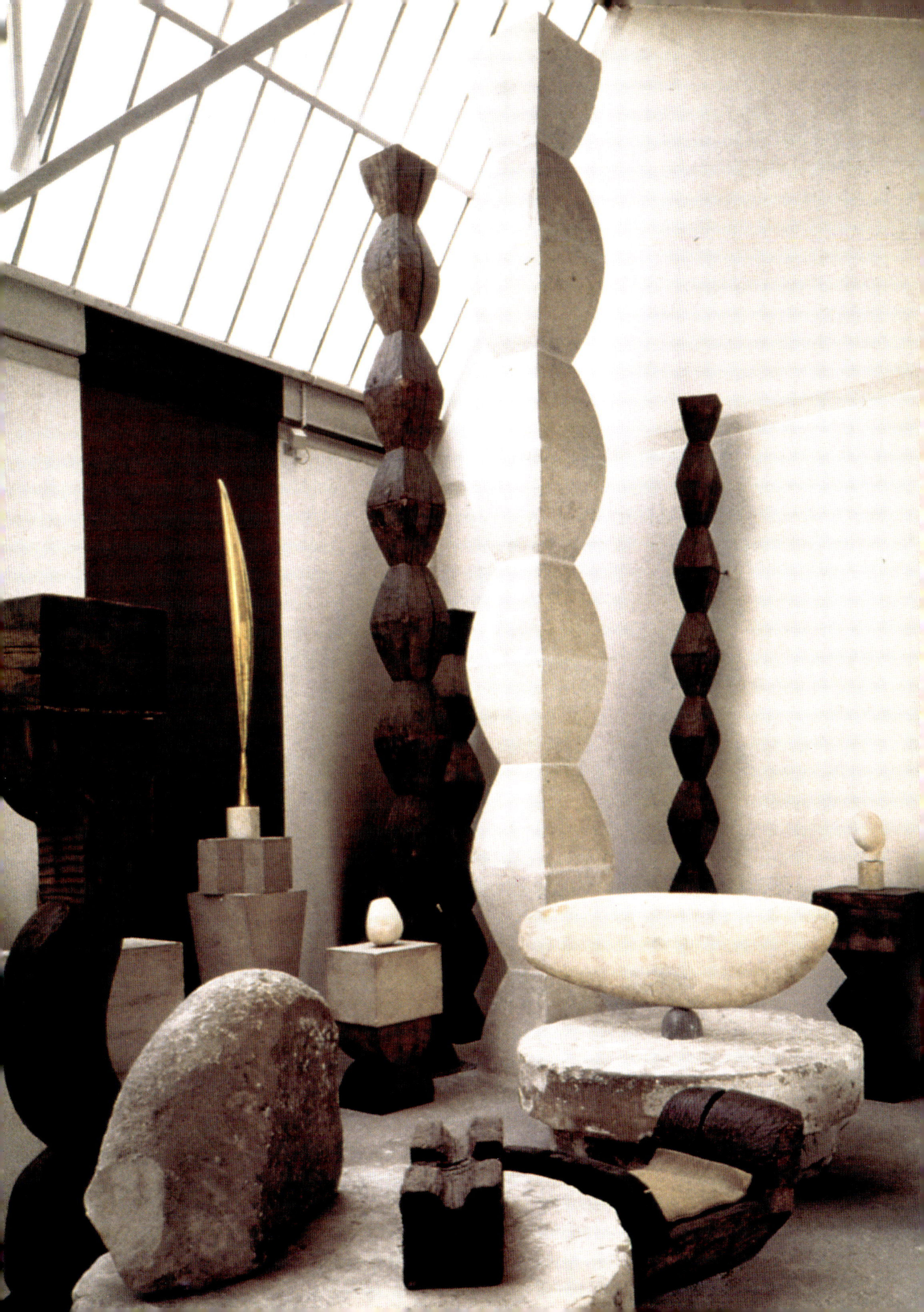

faced with the daunting task of modernizing an overwhelmingly agricultural country with a large rural population. Like many of his countrymen at the time, Brancusi's education coincided with plans put in place by the government to generate a new class of citizens, which would be better equipped to meet the demands of a modern society. Civilization in those days was measured in terms of the social and political transformations brought about by industrial development, what we call modernity today.

Later in life, Brancusi liked to disparage a 'civilization which spoils everything' (to Michel Seuphor, 1949), when reminiscing about his childhood and what he perceived to be the lost innocence of its rural setting. This was definitely rural, but by all accounts it was far from idyllic.

Brancusi's father belonged to the peasant class of small landholders and earned his living managing the estates of the nearby monastery of Tismana. The second of four children with three half-brothers from his father's first marriage, Brancusi found home life so unbearable that he tried to run away on several occasions, finally succeeding aged 11 with only a primary-school education. To support himself, he took on menial jobs in nearby hamlets, including Târgu Jiu. By 1894, Brancusi was living in Craiova, the provincial capital of the Gorj district, where he enrolled, aged 18, in the School of Arts and Crafts. This was the first of a series of training colleges and art schools that Brancusi would attend, thanks to scholarships provided by the state or provincial bodies.

BELOW *L'Écorché* (Flayed Figure), 1902–03, plaster, Institutul de Arte Plastice, 'N. Grigorescu', Bucharest

OPPOSITE Contemporary postcard reproduction of *Torment* in plaster, inscribed by the artist: *Supplice*, Salon 1907, Paris

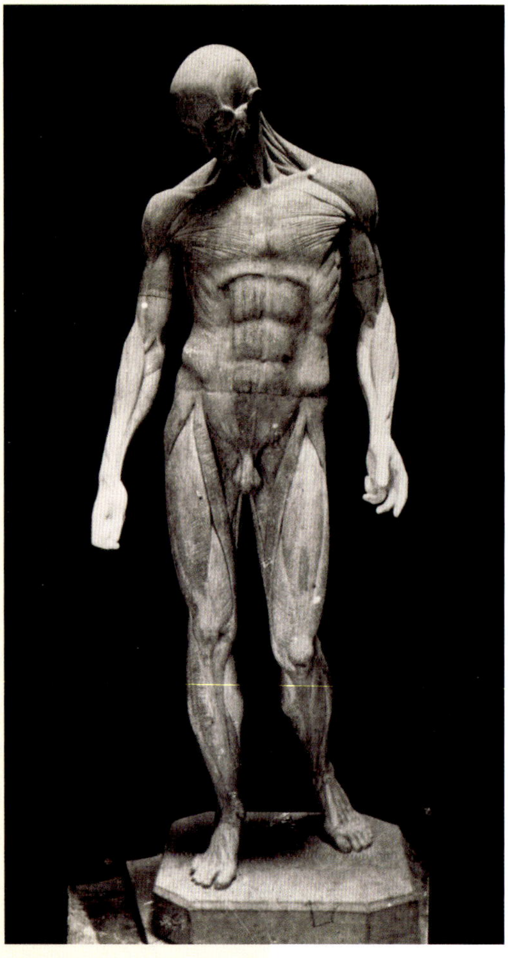

After graduating with honours in 1898, he left for Bucharest and entered the School of Fine Art to study sculpture. The school's curriculum was based on that of the École des Beaux Arts in Paris, where sculpture was considered to be the art form best suited to the task of expressing ideas and moral virtues through the representation of the human figure. For this reason, sculpture was taught predominantly in terms of the figure; this was studied from life models and based on the formal language of classical statuary.

By the end of his course, the extent to which Brancusi had mastered this language is seen in a surviving early work, known as *L'Écorché* (1902–03), meaning flayed or skinned, which was modelled on a genre made famous by the eighteenth-century French artist Jean-Antoine Houdon (1741–1828). This was a life-size representation of the human body and its internal organs mapped on a model of classical statuary, the Capitoline *Antinous*. Plaster copies of this work abounded in the art schools of the time and were used to teach an idealized view of the human body, based on classical proportions. Brancusi executed his version under the supervision of the physician and anatomy professor Dimitrie Gerota.

That Brancusi could win a medal for this work's aesthetic achievement, as well as sell copies to the medical school in Bucharest for use in teaching anatomy, demonstrates the way that art at the time often held a functional purpose beyond simply the aesthetic one of expressing beauty. More importantly, Brancusi was able to use the proceeds from the sale of these works to finance his move to Paris in 1904, a journey he made largely on foot, travelling through Budapest, Vienna and Munich, from May to July of that year.

Turn-of-the-century Paris was the unrivalled capital of the art world and the acknowledged centre for artistic training, which attracted students from across Europe, and from America and Japan. Success in its annual juried salons could secure an aspiring sculptor's reputation and lead to sales and commissions. Thanks to another scholarship, in 1905 Brancusi was able to enrol in Antonin Mercié's sculpture studio at the École des Beaux Arts, a critical step in securing an audience for his work.

Because of age restrictions, Brancusi could study there for only a year. However, the period was long enough for him to gain the support of Mercié, when he began to exhibit his work – mainly busts of children – at the Salon de la Nationale in 1906. At this stage of his development, Brancusi was essentially a gifted copyist excelling in naturalist representation. But Paris and all it had to offer would soon have a profound and lasting effect on his art and outlook, not least in awakening memories of a childhood spent amid woodlands and streams.

PARIS: 'NOTHING CAN GROW IN THE SHADOW OF GREAT TREES'

Brancusi's early financial hardships were somewhat alleviated by the support of a close-knit Romanian community of well-to-do students and artists in Paris, all of whom provided material assistance and introductions to influential people. The most famous of these introductions was to Auguste Rodin (1840–1917), which was facilitated by Otilia Cosmutza, a well-travelled Romanian artist and one-time secretary to Anatole France, a major literary figure of the day.

Rodin was then at the height of his career and was surrounded by a cosmopolitan crowd of admiring artists, writers and collectors. He also ran a large studio employing a number of assistants. Brancusi was invited to join this group sometime in 1907, but he remained in this position for less than a month, stating much later that 'nothing can grow in the shadow of great trees' (in catalogue of IVth *Salon de la jeune sculpture* in Paris, 1952).

These famous words, which refer to Rodin's fame, should not obscure the fact that Brancusi owed much to Rodin's example – in particular, his use of the fragment as an expressive and meaningful element in sculpture. This can be seen in Brancusi's portraits and heads of children at the time. In one, called *Torment* (1906), the expressive body language of the taut neck appears even more poignant because it refers to a child; and this is re-enforced by the work's title.

Brancusi would soon shed this form of illusion and pathos, but he would not readily forget the power that the fragment possessed to communicate meaning, in addition to the already suggestive power of language present in a work's title.

What may have emboldened Brancusi in his decision to leave Rodin so soon was his emerging success as an artist. In the spring of 1907, Brancusi received his first important commission for a funerary monument in a cemetery in the Romanian town of Buzau: the Stanescu Funerary Monument (1910–14). The advance for this work allowed Brancusi to move into his first

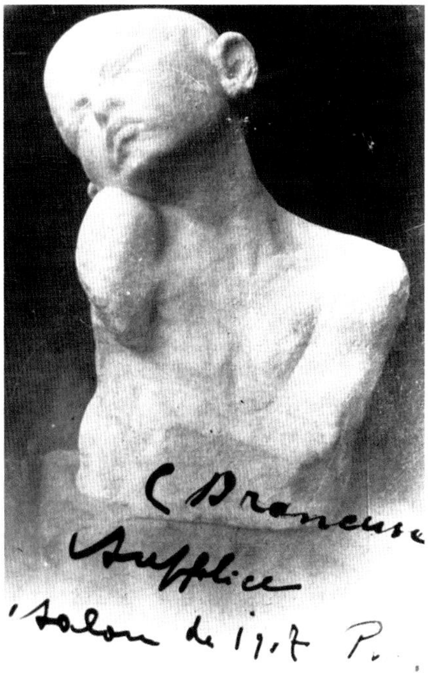

proper studio at 54 rue de Montparnasse. In addition, he was now exhibiting regularly in Paris and Bucharest, where his work was receiving favourable critical attention and was being acquired by Romanian collectors.

One work from this period, *The Kiss* (1909–10), stands out. This was originally created as a funerary monument for the daughter of a Russian family living in Paris, and was erected in the cemetery of Montparnasse in 1910. Brancusi always spoke of this work as his 'road to Damascus', and it marks a watershed in his approach to representation that will continue to inform the abstract imagery of the *Gate* at Târgu Jiu.

The radical stylistic development in this work has always been understood in terms of the technique used: direct carving as opposed to modelling in clay, and transferral to stone by a skilled technician, often by means of a pointing machine (a three-dimensional pantograph, which enabled an

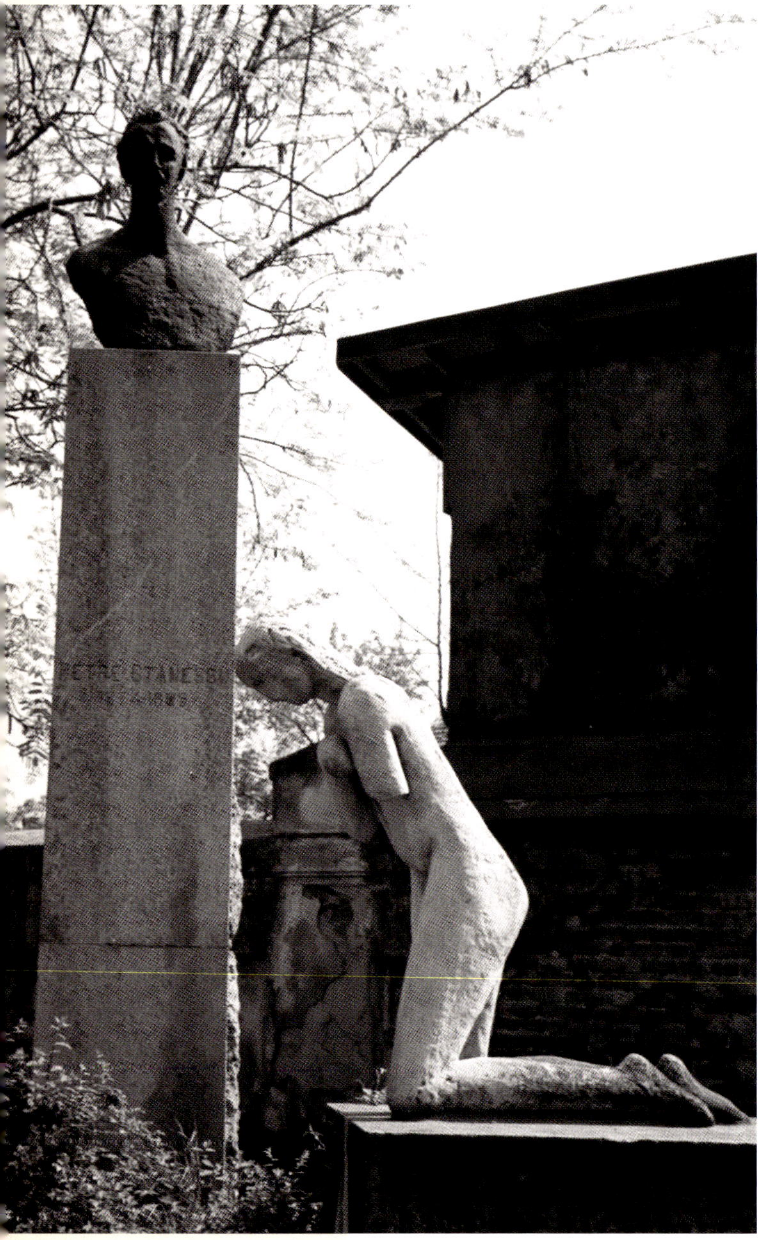

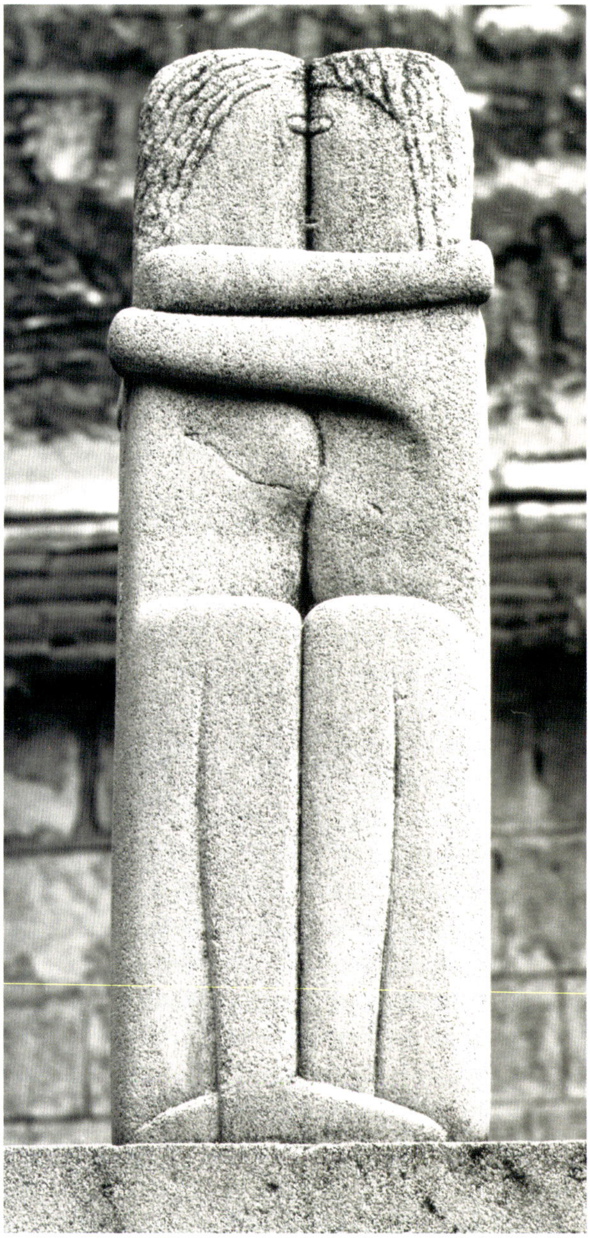

BELOW LEFT Stanescu Funerary Monument, 1907–14, showing *Portrait of Petre Stanescu* and *The Prayer*, bronze and stone, in Buzau Cemetery

BELOW RIGHT *The Kiss* 1909–10, stone, in Montparnasse Cemetery, Paris

OPPOSITE *Maiastra*, 1911. Bronze and stone, Tate Modern, London. Acquired 1973 almost exact replication or enlargement from any original work). *The Kiss* was indeed carved directly – but in stone, a material that was coarse-grained and far less luminous than marble. Such a material precluded the depiction of elaborate gestures or surface textures that gave the illusion of living flesh, such as in Rodin's *Kiss* (1898).

Brancusi's *Kiss* was a much simpler image, in which the figures, reduced to a basic schema, appear contained within the stone. What was really taking place, however, was a radical change in the perception of representation and its fundamental mechanisms, which led, above all, to the shedding of the notion that representation should imitate natural forms.

The view that 'direct carving' alone is what distinguished Brancusi's approach to sculpture from Rodin's, is to confuse a technical process with an approach to imagery. The source of confusion lies in traditional notions of sculpture based on classical statuary and the latter's close connection to naturalism, which was regarded at the time as the only means to represent reality faithfully. The force of this tradition obscures the basic fact that it is only a convention, or one approach to representation, among many.

Brancusi came to this realization gradually. What may have influenced him were the arts of non-western and pre-classical societies that he encountered in Paris. At the time, such works were beginning to be appreciated by critics and collectors for their ability to convey meaning without having recourse to realistic imitation. Thus, when Brancusi made this inference, considering his long practice in copying, one can assume it was not difficult for him to forego any concern with imitation and the illusions of reality, in his approach to making art and objects.

Brancusi's work from this period reflects the wide range of cultural artefacts that he encountered on visits to exhibitions and museums, and which, in turn, he was exploring in his work. Egyptian art, for instance, offered one alternative to imitation due to its stylized and emblematic approach to form, which Brancusi adopted in *Maiastra* (1911). The frontal viewpoint and rigid organization of this work focus on a bird's essential features (an elongated head and neck, a round torso framed by what appears to be its gathered plumage) and impart to the form a hieratic appearance. Notwithstanding this, it was certainly easier to abandon realistic imagery when dealing with animals, as these already featured in stylized form in all manner of decorations as well as in folk art.

However, Egyptian art was also valued for the mysterious rituals it was thought to serve. As its exact iconography and meaning had not yet been deciphered, Egyptian art was held to be 'mysterious' and provided artists and writers of the period with a form of imagery that they needed to express alternative paths to spirituality. This was often located in the representation of light, which was believed to have transformative powers. Thus, Egyptian art provided a fitting style for a sculpture like *Maiastra*, whose title was drawn from Romanian folklore. Maiastra is the name of the golden bird with supernatural powers, which appears at revelatory moments to guide heroes through perilous journeys.

Can we assume, then, that the *Maiastra* held both formal and symbolic

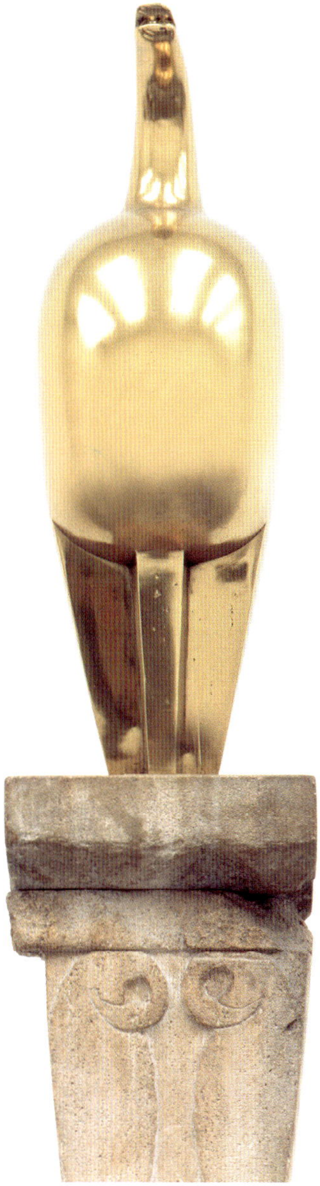

values? Brancusi's own Orthodox faith may have predisposed him to a more mystical approach to art; and it has been argued that, long after he had shed this type of explicit iconography, he would retain golden surfaces in his works. These were obtained through direct polish of the bronze material and signalled the role that light was to play in his mature work as a meaningful concept to understand form.

In Paris, accompanied by Otilia Cosmutza, Brancusi would visit the recently opened Musée Guimet, which housed a collection of manuscripts from Tibet as well as Far-Eastern statuary and figures of Buddha. This art had a profound effect on Brancusi's treatment of facial features, particularly in works like *Sleeping Muse* (1910) and *Mademoiselle Pogany* (1912), the first of a series that originated as a portrait of a young Hungarian friend, who later described the work as being 'all eyes'. In addition, the treatment of the arms in this figure, as virtually a separate element made to stand in for the entire torso, owes something to Rodin's approach to figures assembled from independently modelled body parts.

> 'The extreme freedom of Paris has allowed Brancusi to remain the least "Parisian" of artists, and what is indeed rarer still, the least "Parisian" of Romanians' (Paul Morand, Brummer Gallery catalogue, 1926)

Mademoiselle Pogany (version I, 1913, after a marble of 1912). Museum of Modern Art (MoMA), New York. Bronze, 43.8 x 21.5 x 31.7 cm, on limestone base, 14.6 x 15.6 x 18.7 cm. Acquired through the Lillie P. Bliss Bequest. 2.1953

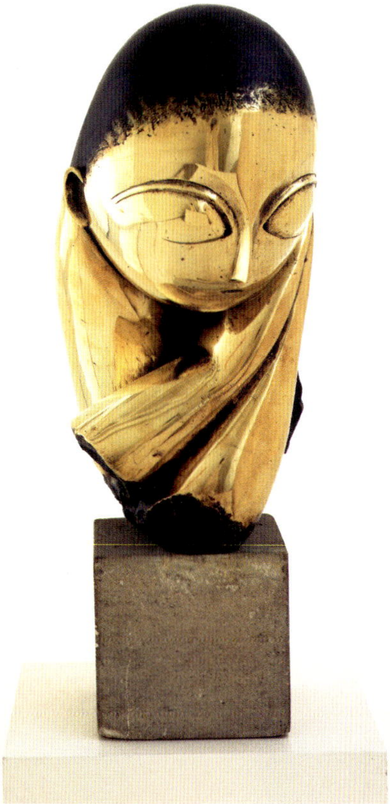

To gain a fuller picture of the artist who worked at Târgu Jiu, we need to understand more about the way his career progressed and the circumstances that contributed to the development of his ideas.

Although Brancusi could claim a significant number of friends in the Parisian art world – including painters, sculptors and writers like Henri Rousseau (1812–67), Amedeo Modigliani (1884–1920), Fernand Léger (1881–1955), Marcel Duchamp (1887–1968), Francis Picabia (1879–1953) and Guillaume Apollinaire (1880–1918) – his big breakthrough came with the invitation to participate in the 1913 International Exhibition of Modern Art, in New York, more commonly known as The Armory Show.

This was largely due to the American photographer Edward Steichen (1879–1973), who had met Brancusi through Rodin and had recently acquired a bronze version of the 1911 *Maiastra* (now in the Tate Modern in London). Brancusi sent five works to The Armory Show, all of which were sold; the following year, he was given his first one-man show by the photographer Alfred Stieglitz (1864–1946), in his Photo-Secession Gallery in New York. This helped to establish Brancusi's reputation among American collectors.

In a sense, Brancusi was following again in the footsteps of Rodin, who was much admired by Stieglitz and his circle. But Brancusi was now emerging as an artist who was pushing the boundaries of art and producing work that would become, for Americans, exemplary – perhaps even *the* symbol of modern art.

America represented a turning point for Brancusi, because there he was able to secure the patronage of a small but devoted group of distinguished collectors who acquired his work on a regular basis. The American lawyer

John Quinn, who acquired 27 sculptures between 1914 and 1924, is probably the most important of these; he is followed by Katherine Dreier, whose collection – built on the advice of Duchamp – would be bequeathed to Yale University. Another important collector was Walter Arensberg, also a friend of Duchamp, whose collection would form the cornerstone of the Philadelphia Museum of Art's Duchamp and Brancusi holdings.

Friends of Brancusi, such as Steichen, Duchamp and Henri-Pierre Roché, sometimes acted as intermediaries. In the case of Duchamp and Steichen, this commercial relationship would blossom into a significant creative exchange and a lasting friendship. Soon Brancusi would come to rely almost exclusively on intermediaries for promoting and selling his work. In turn, the financial security and ready market allowed him sufficient freedom to explore new ideas. This resulted in a whole body of work that was created and viewed in the privacy of his Parisian studio.

Our current understanding of Brancusi's development as an artist is often seen in the context of its public reception, which often led to controversies. Although these provide valuable insight into the public sensibility of the period, they should not be confused with the artist's intentions nor regarded as explanations of his work.

Two separate events illustrate this point: firstly, the scandal that arose in Paris in 1920 when Brancusi sent a bronze version of his 1916 *Princesse X* to an official exhibiting body, the Salon des Artistes Indépendants; and, secondly, the controversy in 1926 that emerged after one of his works – *Bird in Space* (1926), owned by Steichen – was refused duty-free entry into the USA by customs officials, who argued that it was not a work of art.

In the case of *Princesse X*, the piece was forcibly removed from public display by French authorities, who believed the sculpture resembled a phallus. They ignored Brancusi's claims that the bust was the result of a long process of simplification and refinement of a naturalistic marble bust of a woman. He even produced a photograph of the earlier work to support his claim.

Such controversies took place at a time when some of Brancusi's closest friends, including Duchamp, Picabia and the Romanian poet Tristan Tzara (1896–1963), were actively looking to upset bourgeois complacency by attacking conventional attitudes about art and propriety. These activities were performed in the name of Dada, the controversial art movement that had originated in Zurich in 1916 as a protest against the futility of war. While it is known that Brancusi sympathized with some Dadaist ideas, it is unclear whether he knowingly sent *Princesse X* to the Salon with the sole purpose of offending the authorities.

Bird in Space was refused tax-free entry (despite being indeed a work of art), because the work's abstracted and elongated form did not resemble a real bird – at least to the customs official. This event resulted in a famous court case that concerned the definition of modern art, which Brancusi (assisted by Duchamp and Steichen) brought against US Customs in New York in 1927. In 1928, the court exonerated Brancusi when the judge declared *Bird in Space* to be a work of art, by extending the definition of art to cover works not resembling reality. This victory did little, however, to explain to

Princesse X, 1916. Bronze. Musée national d'art moderne, Centre Pompidou, Paris

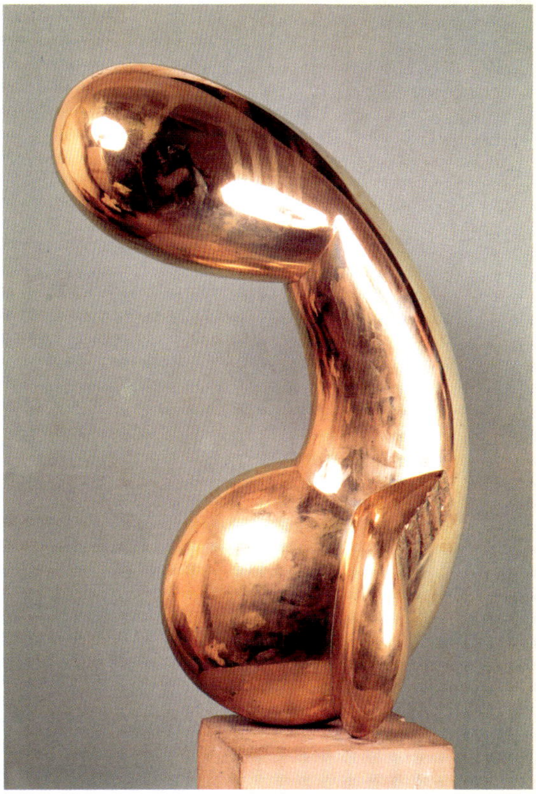

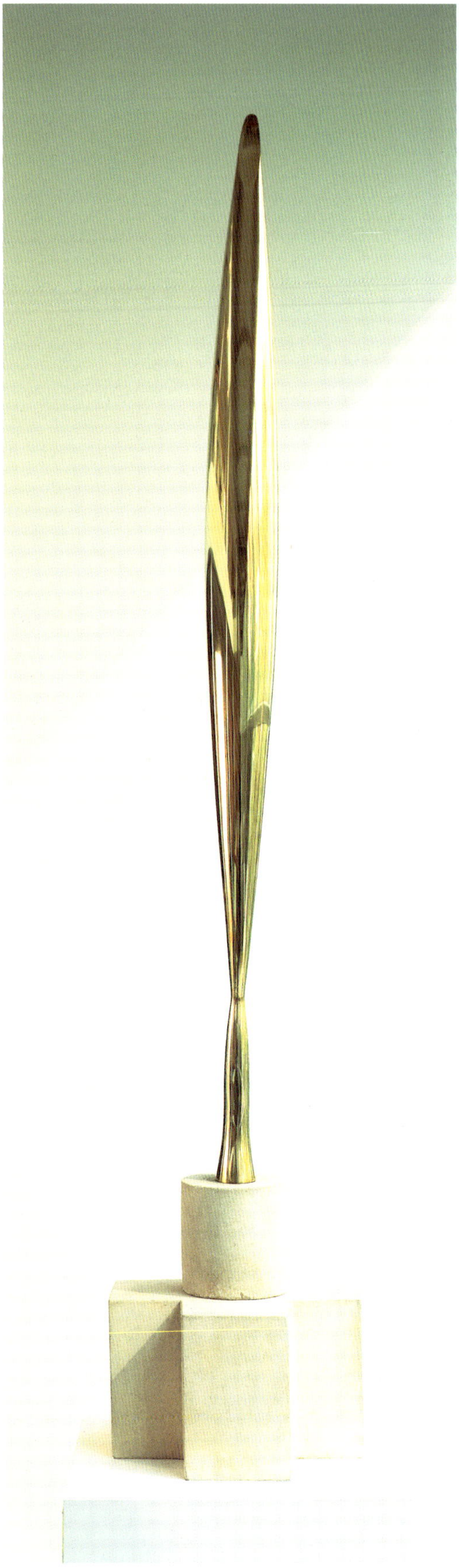

the public the experience that Brancusi wished to convey through his work.

Both events show that many viewers found the growing abstraction of Brancusi's formal language difficult to comprehend. Confronted with his work, they could see it only through conventions of representation with which they were familiar, namely that a work of art imitated and resembled 'reality'.

> 'One arrives at simplicity in spite of oneself, in approaching the real sense of things' (Constantin Brancusi, Brummer Gallery catalogue, 1926)

The court case involving *Bird in Space* brought to public attention a way of creating art that defined Brancusi's approach, which was to work and rework a form to produce a series of different versions of a given subject. To explain this method of working, and to appreciate how Brancusi used these conventions to his own advantage, we need to be aware of conventional practices within the field.

Traditional market strategies to sell sculpture in the nineteenth and early twentieth centuries relied on the production of popular subjects, which were then replicated using mechanical means, in various sizes and materials according to demand; Rodin was an artist who worked in this way. Brancusi, though, turned this practice into a creative exercise that is better understood when compared to the approach adopted by painters working in series like Claude Monet (1840–1926).

A series becomes an exploration of a given motif, instead of an exploitation of that motif. For some, Brancusi's work appears to be a series of abstractions from the initial naturalistic model, similar to Matisse's series of *Backs* (1909–1930). But Brancusi seems to be looking for the best expression of an idea through form, which is never entirely abstract. He makes use of titles that carry traces of subject matter and are meant to bridge the gap between a form and its meaning. He also took up photography, first as a means of promoting his work with collectors, then as an artistic medium. This allowed him to compose elaborate tableaux of his sculptures and their studio setting, while playing with dramatic perspective and light effects.

Brancusi's Paris studio, like many sculptors' studios, doubled as his showroom. However, what made his so distinctive was the environment he created in that space. Brancusi's studio contained only his own artworks; he was not a collector like Rodin, of classical or Far-Eastern statuary, and he did not acquire African masks, as did Pablo Picasso (1881–1973) or Henri Matisse (1869–1954). Brancusi's sculptures were displayed in a setting fashioned from his imagination and made by his own hands, on an assortment of wooden or stone carved bases, or under wooden arches.

The Târgu Jiu *Endless Column (Colonne sans Fin)* and the *Table of Silence* originated in this space, and they belong to those areas of sculpture that had become very formulaic and bland: namely, the pedestals or bases. With Brancusi, the bases took on a charge that sought to integrate these elements into the work, to provide a frame and to establish metaphorically a visual connec-

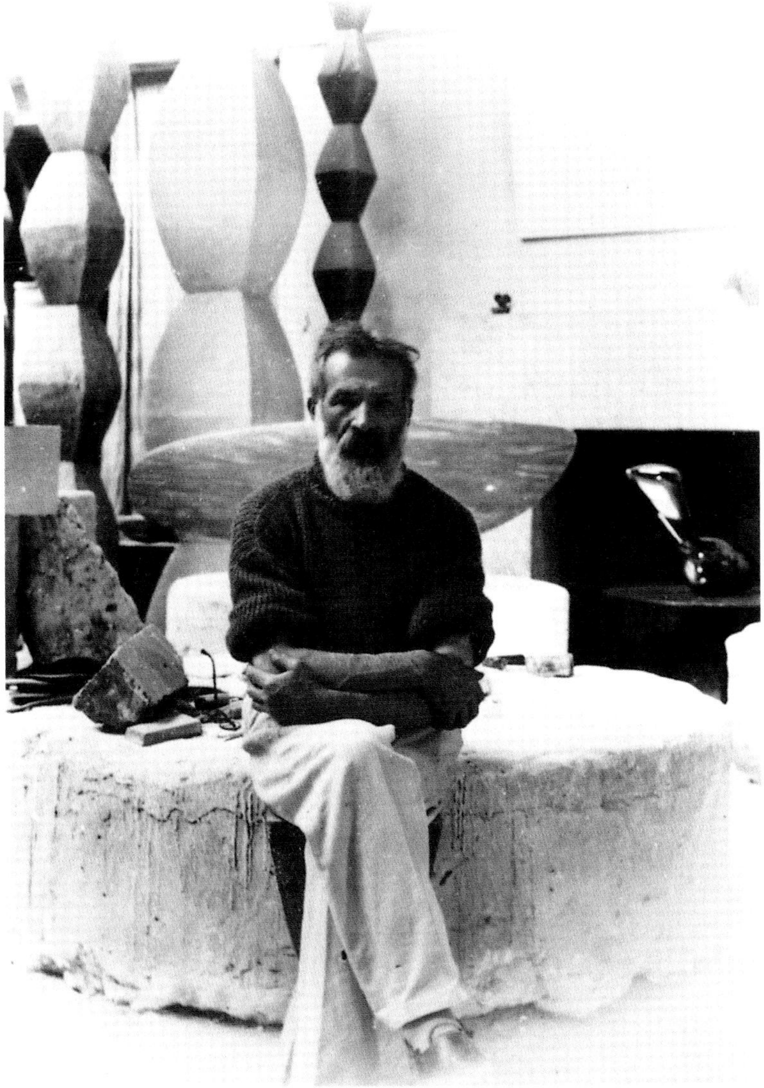

OPPOSITE *Bird in Space*, 1928. Bronze (unique cast), 137.2 x 21.6 x 16.5 cm. Museum of Modern Art (MoMA), New York. Given anonymously. 153.1934. This version was not the one involved in the court case

LEFT *Self-Portrait in the studio*, c.1934, showing versions I–IV of the *Endless Column* and *Fish*. Constantin Brancusi Bequest, 1957. Musée national d'art moderne, Centre Pompidou, Paris

tion, which linked the sculpture to the ground. Though both these forms evolved in outline and proportion, their basic shape remained unchanged when they appeared again at Târgu Jiu.

Stylistic sources for the *Column* have been sought in African art and Romanian peasant art, which Brancusi had looked at with increased attention from his mid-teens, often playing one so-called 'primitive art' against the other. Wood and particularly aged oak, which Brancusi recycled from old building beams, was still an unusual choice of material for a work of art. But it was one that Brancusi particularly liked handling.

The earliest *Column*, dated 1917 (now in the collection of the Museum of Modern Art in New York), measures just over two-metres high and was carved from a single block of oak. Despite its diminutive size, it encompasses all the features that would become the hallmark of Brancusi's subsequent columns: a series of equal rhomboidal units and the characteristic half-unit at either end.

It is extraordinary how, at such an early stage, Brancusi had arrived at the simple yet elegant solution to express visually the concept of the infinite.

The half-units keep the mind alert to their potential wholeness, and thus provide the illusion of a form with no fixed limits. When this first *Column* was sold to Quinn in 1917, Brancusi described the work, in a letter to the collector, as both a sculpture and a sign for an ideal environment with which to surround his other works.

In 1920, Brancusi explored the form on a larger scale when he erected another column in the garden of Steichen's home in Voulangis, outside Paris. This one was carved out of a single tree trunk measuring five-and-a-half metres.

In its outdoor setting amid trees and vegetation, Steichen's *Column* could be regarded as 'art imitating nature' and as expressing the ethos of 'truth to material'. However, this detracts only from the fact that we are dealing with a representation or, in other words, an aesthetic object firmly rooted in the *man-made* world and therefore separate from the trees and rocks found in nature.

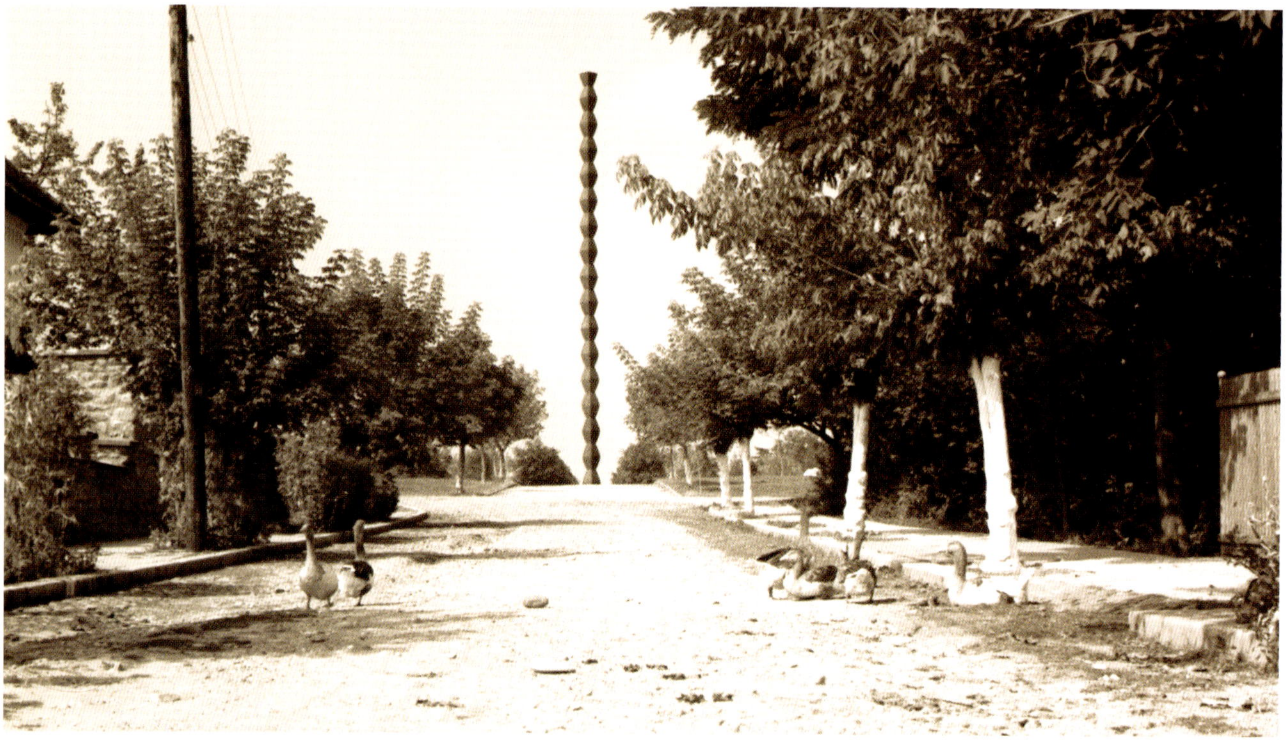

The title *Column without End* (now *Endless Column*) first appears in 1926, in the catalogue of Brancusi's first exhibition at the Brummer Gallery in New York, as a designation for Quinn's 1917 *Column* (one of the works being sold). When he showed the Steichen *Column* and other wood columns at another Brummer exhibition (1933), Brancusi added a cosmic note to this title: 'Project of columns which, when enlarged, will support the arch of the firmament.'

Each of these designations reinforces the notion that Brancusi considered the form's representation, and the space it occupies, in architectural rather than organic terms. Here is where any interpretation of the *Endless Column* as a monumental sculpture must begin.

By the 1930s, Brancusi was considering making a number of his works on a larger scale, and described them as such in the entries of his 1933 Brummer exhibition catalogue. For example, the plaster *Column of the Kiss* (begun in 1916) was listed there as a 'project for the Temple of Love'; the large *Birds* were to 'fill the vault of the sky'. When the Târgu Jiu commission arose in 1935, it could not have come at a better moment for Brancusi, who was ready to embark on a large-scale project – and, moreover, he was given the opportunity to make it his own.

The commission came from an unlikely source of patronage: Aretie Tatarescu, who was president of the National League of Gorj Women (a charitable organization) and also the wife of a prominent Romanian politician. The subject was highly conventional: a war memorial dedicated to the memory of World War I soldiers from the Gorj region, men who died while

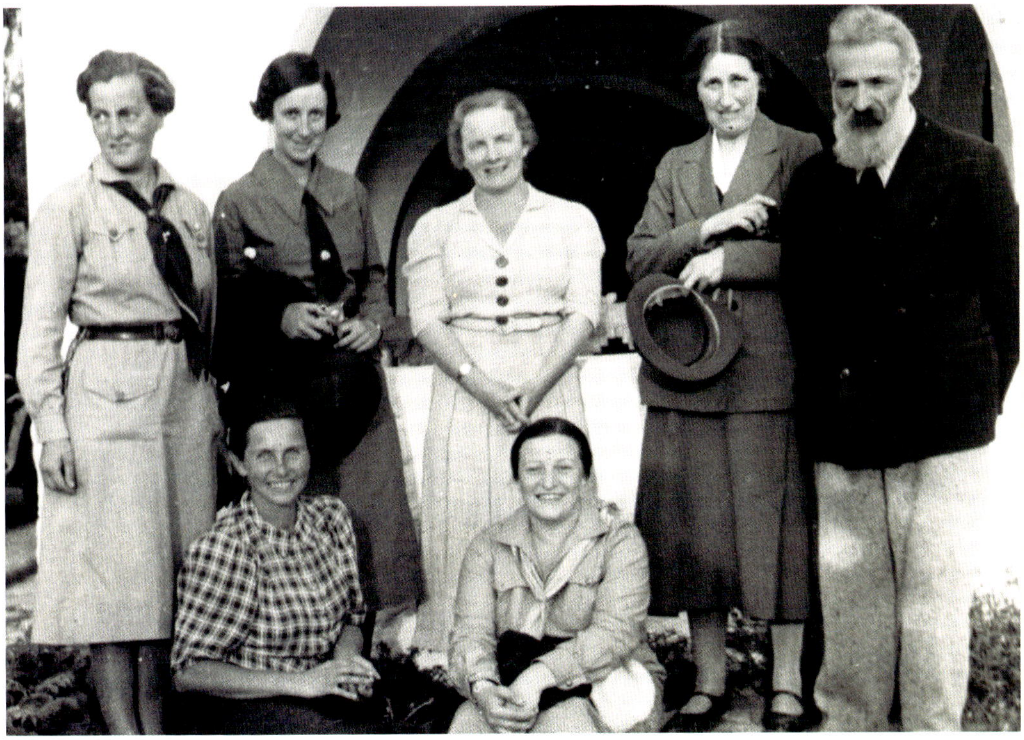

OPPOSITE View of Avenue of the Heroes and *Endless Column*, Târgu Jiu, c.1940s

LEFT Aretie Tatarescu (centre), Brancusi and members of the National League of Gorj Women at the Tatarescu residence in Poiană, outside Târgu Jiu, 1937

fighting the Germans in November 1916. But Tatarescu's choice of artist was unexpected as this was a genre of sculpture that Brancusi particularly abhorred.

It appears that Brancusi only got involved with this patron through another Romanian artist, Militsa Petrascu (1892–1975), who had befriended the sculptor in Paris in the 1920s, when she was studying art in the city. Petrascu had recently completed a commission for the League – a small monument in the centre of Târgu Jiu, dedicated to the memory of a World War I heroine, Ecaterinei Teodoroiu. Petrascu had been invited to create the larger war memorial, but had turned this down, saying that it surpassed her abilities. As an alternative, she suggested Brancusi, her friend and mentor.

Brancusi's reply to Petrascu in a letter, dated 11 February 1935, is a touching testimony to the importance he attached to this invitation and the opportunity it gave him to return to his homeland: 'Now all my works, embarked upon a long time ago, are reaching their end. I feel something like an apprentice on the eve of his graduation, thus the commission could not have come at a better time.' (*Actuellement tous mes ouvrages commencés depuis si longtemps touchent à leur fin et je me sens tel l'apprenti à la veille de devenir ouvrier – donc la proposition ne pouvait mieux tomber.*)

Tatarescu visited Brancusi in his studio in Paris and was interested in the artist's large sculptures of cockerels, which are the symbol of the Oltenia region in Romania, which includes Târgu Jiu. It was also a motif found on carpets that were woven in the League's workshops, based on Tatarescu's own designs. But Brancusi regarded the cockerel as a French subject, referring to it as 'le Coq Gallique', and he insisted instead on proposing a column as a fitting subject for the Târgu Jiu commission.

This abstract form was a highly unusual choice for a monument in the 1930s; in fact, Brancusi had already attempted to have a column erected in Bucharest in 1930, but without success (according to an article in the Romanian daily, *Curentul*, of 6 October 1930). At this date, the prevailing opinion in Romania was that monuments had to convey an intelligible message through figurative representation.

The *Endless Column's* unconventionality can be measured by comparing it with Petrascu's own monument at Târgu Jiu, which was well received and which reflected the stylized figuration that was considered to be modern back then. This was a stone structure in the form of a sarcophagus, flanked on each corner by large female figures representing peasant women. Each face was decorated with shallow reliefs depicting scenes from the *Mioritsa*, a famous Romanian folk tale whose symbolism of sacrificial death and rebirth was familiar to all.

The successful outcome of Brancusi's project at Târgu Jiu was undoubtedly facilitated by the artist's good relations with his patron Aretie Tatarescu. Brancusi refused to accept any payment for his work, and no formal contract for the commission survives. Tatarescu managed the entire project, including overseeing construction and payments to contractors.

Furthermore, she was able to call on powerful friends to lend significant financial and material support. The industrialist Ion Malaxa donated the iron ore used for the *Endless Column*; Ion Bujoi, as President of the Societate Anonima Romana pentru Exploatarea Minelor de Carbuni, paid for the casting and labour. It must have helped that her husband, Georghe Tatarescu, who was Prime Minister from 1934 to 1937, had his parliamentary seat in the Gorj district.

Another factor that aided the successful outcome of the project was probably the remoteness of Târgu Jiu, a small market town in Oltenia, which was far from the capital and therefore far from possible adverse criticism. Târgu Jiu was also a place where the National League of Gorj Women was the most generous and respected philanthropic institution.

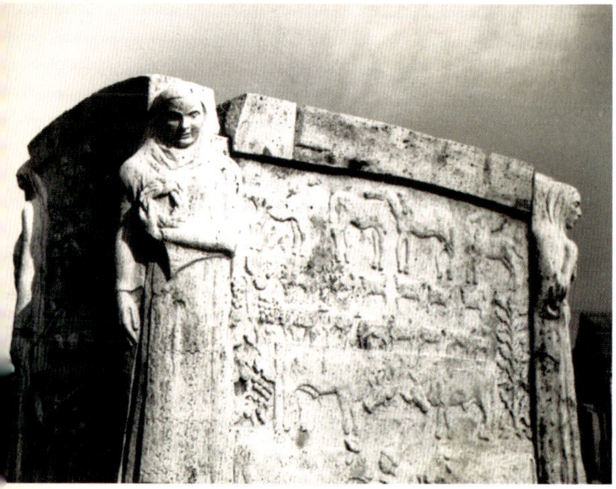

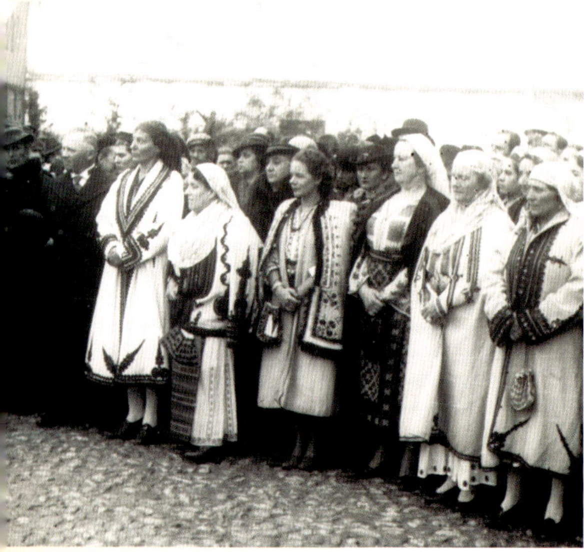

TOP Militsa Petrascu, *Monument to Ecaterinei Teodoroiu*, 1935, Târgu Jiu

ABOVE Militsa Petrascu (second from left), Sanda Tatarescu-Negropontes and Aretie Tatarescu (second from right), and members of the National League of Gorj Women at the consecration ceremony of Petrascu's monument, 1935

Although Brancusi accepted the commission in 1935, two years would elapse before construction began in 1937. Measuring 30-metres high, the *Endless Column* at Târgu Jiu was the most ambitious project that Brancusi had undertaken; it differed not only in size from his previous columns but also in its material, which was metal rather than wood.

To help with technical issues, Brancusi enlisted the help of Stefan Georgescu-Gorjan, the son of an old friend and an engineer at the steel company Atelierele Centrale Petrosani (The Petrosani Central Workshops), north of Târgu Jiu, which would cast the *Column*. It is known that Georgescu-Gorjan played a crucial role in helping Brancusi find the appropriate technical means to translate his ideas; although it is generally believed that Gorjan suggested using a series of hollow elements strung on a central core or pillar for the *Column*, there is some debate about this. For a detailed account of this aspect of the commission see the next chapter.

One crucial issue they faced was the surface finish of the cast-iron modules, which had to be coated for protection against rust. Brancusi had repeatedly insisted that this metal coating be as 'yellow' as possible. Brass (or *laiton* in French) had been Brancusi's metal of choice for his polished bronze sculptures like *Bird in Space*, as it produced a beautiful golden colour. However, obtaining a similar effect on a work that would be exposed to the elements was a challenge.

The correspondence between Brancusi, Gorjan and Aretie Tatarescu shows that the company Metalizarea, which was in charge of this aspect of the project, advised strongly against using brass, because the material oxidized over time and turned an unpleasant dark colour. In its place, Metalizarea recommended bronze or even copper, although the latter tended to be more reddish than the desired yellow. Samples were made in both materials, but there is no surviving written evidence confirming the final choice. This question would remain a controversial issue for all subsequent restorations of the *Column*.

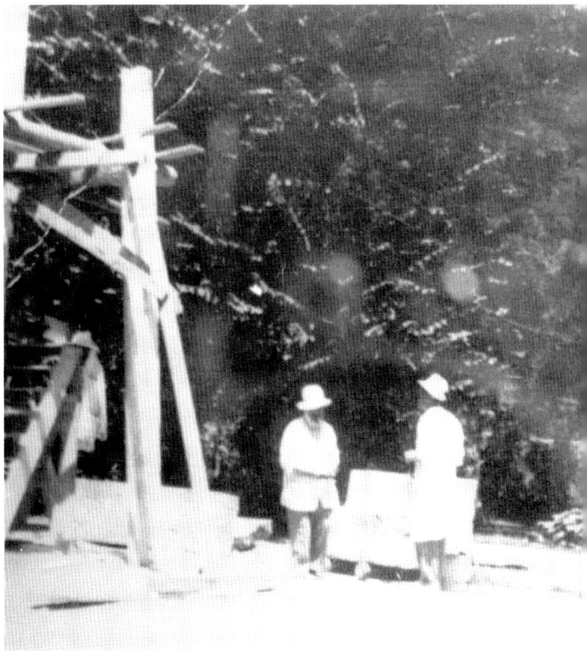

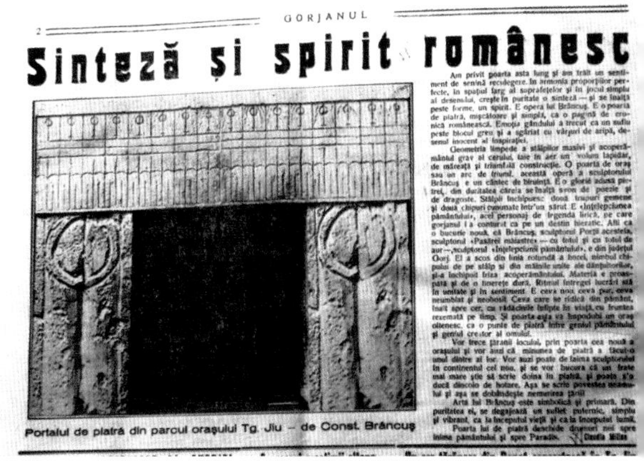

GORJANUL

Sinteză şi spirit românesc

Portalul de piatră din parcul oraşului Tg. Jiu – de Const. Brâncuş

Am privit poarta asta lung şi am trăit un sentiment de senină reculegere. În armonia proporţiilor perfecte, în spaţiul larg al suprafeţelor şi în jocul simplu al desenului, creşte în puritate o sinteză — şi se înalţă peste forme, un spirit. E opera lui Brâncuş. E o poartă de piatră, mişcătoare şi simplă, ca o pagină de cronică românească. Emoţia gândului a trecut ca un suflu peste blocul greu şi a sgâriat cu vârfuri de aripă, desenul inocent al inspiraţiei.

Geometria limpede a stâlpilor masivi şi acoperământul grav al cerului, taie în aer un volum lapidar, de măreaţă şi triumfală construcţie. O poartă de oraş sau un arc de triumf, această operă a sculptorului Brâncuş e un cântec de biruinţă. E o glorie adusă pietrei, din duritatea căreia se înalţă svon de poezie şi de dragoste. Stâlpii închipuesc două trupuri gemene şi două chipuri cununate într'un sărut. E «Înţelepciunea pământului», acel personaj de legendă lirică, pe care gorjanul l-a conturat ca pe un destin hieratic. Aflu ca o bucurie nouă, că Brâncuş, sculptorul Porţii acesteia, sculptorul «Pasărei măiastre» — cu totul şi cu totul de aur —, sculptorul «Înţelepciunii pământului», e din judeţul Gorj. El a scos din linia rotundă a boltei, nimbul chipului de pe stâlp şi din mâinile unite ale dănţuitorilor, şi-a închipuit friza acoperământului. Materia e proaspătă şi de o tinereţe dură. Ritmul întregei lucrări stă în unitate şi în sentiment. E ceva nou, ceva pur, ceva neumblat şi neobosit. Ceva care se ridică din pământ, înalt spre cer, cu rădăcinile înfipte în viaţă, cu fruntea rezemată pe timp. Şi poarta aşa va împodobi un oraş oltenesc, ca o punte de piatră între geniul pământului şi geniul creator al omului.

Vor trece ţăranii locului, prin poarta cea nouă a oraşului şi vor auzi că minunea de piatră a făcut-o unul dintre ai lor. Vor auzi poate de faima sculptorului în continentul cel nou, şi se vor bucura că un frate mai mare ştie să scrie doina în piatră, şi poate s'o ducă dincolo de hotare. Aşa se scrie povestea neamului şi aşa se dobândeşte nemurirea ţării.

Arta lui Brâncuş este simbolică şi primară. Din puritatea ei, se degajează un suflet puternic, simplu şi vibrant, ca la începutul vieţii şi ca la începutul lumii.

Poarta lui de piatră deschide drumuri noi spre inima pământului şi spre Paradis. Claudia Millian

TOP Brancusi and Ion Alexandrescu, the stonecutter, at work near the *Gate of the Kiss* in the park of Târgu Jiu, 1938

ABOVE Claudia Millian article, *Sinteză şi spirit românesc*, in *Gorjanul*, 8 Nov. 1937, illustrating the plaster maquette of the *Gate of the Kiss*

THE INADVERTENT MAKING OF A MONUMENTAL ENSEMBLE

The first mention of a 'monumental gate' appeared in a town hall memorandum dated 2 October 1937, which also lists all the works commissioned by the League 'to glorify the memory of the Gorjan Heroes'. According to this, a 'column' and a 'stone portal' would mark the newly created road called Avenue of the Heroes, which would run from the banks of the River Jiu through the public garden and join the site of the completed building of the Church of the Apostles Peter and Paul. These documents have always led to the assumption that both the *Column* and the *Gate* were commissioned at the same time, and that a monumental ensemble was planned at Târgu Jiu from the beginning.

According to Tatarescu's daughter, Sanda Tatarescu-Negropontes, however, this was not the case. Brancusi had expressed interest in her mother's beautification projects while staying as a guest with their family at their estate in Poianà, outside Târgu Jiu, in June 1937. This interest included the design of a gate for the Public Gardens. The surviving correspondence between Brancusi, Gorjan and Tatarescu supports this version of events: by September 1937, Brancusi had not yet sent the definitive designs or any measurements, which were needed for ordering material for the stone gate (*portii de piatra*).

On the other hand, a surviving undated draft letter from Brancusi to Tatarescu (written in Paris), states that he proposed having the location of the *Gate* moved to a site inside the garden. Brancusi explained that, 'had it remained along the pavement, it would have served no use whatsoever, neither to close the garden nor to be viewed as a separate object in its own right'. This suggests that Brancusi was not only taking over the design of an entrance gate but that he also intended to transform it into an entirely different project, which would become what is now known as the *Gate of the Kiss*.

At some point, Brancusi executed a small model of the *Gate* in plaster, carving one of the small piers in stone and replicating the other in plaster. He photographed the model and sent the pictures to officials in Târgu Jiu with some sketches. This photograph appeared in the local paper, *Gorjanul*, in November 1937, and has led some scholars to conclude mistakenly that the *Gate* was finished in 1937. In fact, only the foundations were in place at the time of the ceremonies consecrating the Church of the Apostles Peter and Paul in October, 1937.

At some point, either when he returned for the ceremonies or more likely in 1938, when work on the *Gate* took place, Brancusi brought to Târgu Jiu the model's plaster lintel and one of the pillars. He subsequently left these as gifts for friends.

How the final piece in this ensemble, the *Table of Silence*, came about, remains a mystery. There is no mention in the records of a commission or a donation, although the town archives contain order forms, dating from August 1938, for stone blocks from the nearby Deva stone workshop. The archives also list a number of stone benches and seats, which had been ordered to furnish the park, although we do not know if they were ordered by the League or the Mayor's office.

The *Table* appears to have evolved out of this aspect of the project. What is certain is that Brancusi was personally involved with the *Table*, and that it was designed with a specific location in mind: the edge of the River Jiu, close to the place where the battle had been fought and so many soldiers had died.

According to eye witnesses, the *Table* went through several permutations before reaching its present proportions (blocks that were discarded from this process can be found nearby today). An inscription naming Brancusi as the artist was placed on the *Table*; this horrified the sculptor, who did not want any form of signage and had the inscription removed.

Brancusi initially envisaged placing the seats around this table in pairs, before settling on the final symmetrical layout. Ion Alexandrescu, the stonemason in charge of carving the motifs on the *Gate*, recalls being asked by Brancusi to sit on one of the seats so the sculptor could calculate the distance necessary to ensure that one's knees did not touch the *Table*. Brancusi did not

Anonymous, *Brancusi at Târgu Jiu*, after July 1937. View of the artist in front of the future site of the *Endless Column*, with Brancusi's sketch of the *Column* drawn in. Constantin Brancusi Bequest, 1957. Musée national d'art moderne, Centre Pompidou, Paris

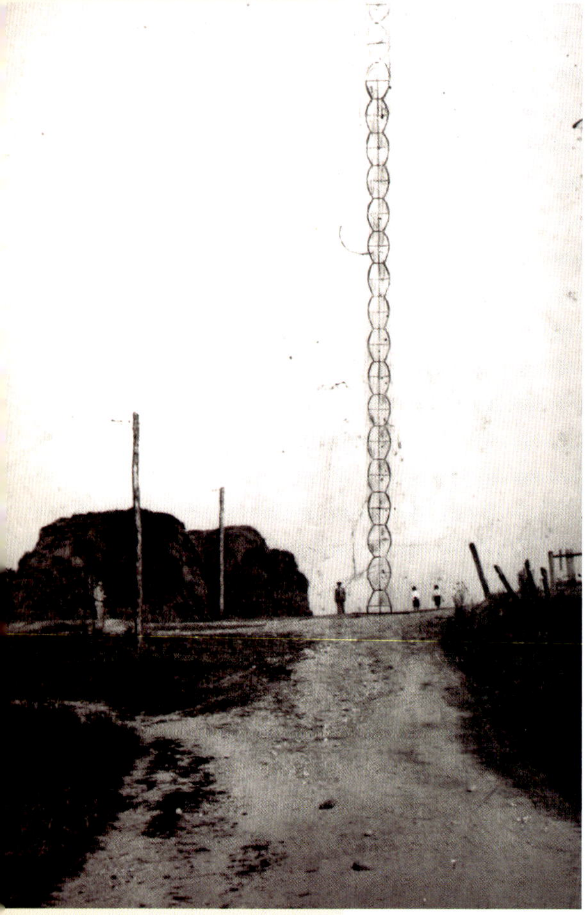

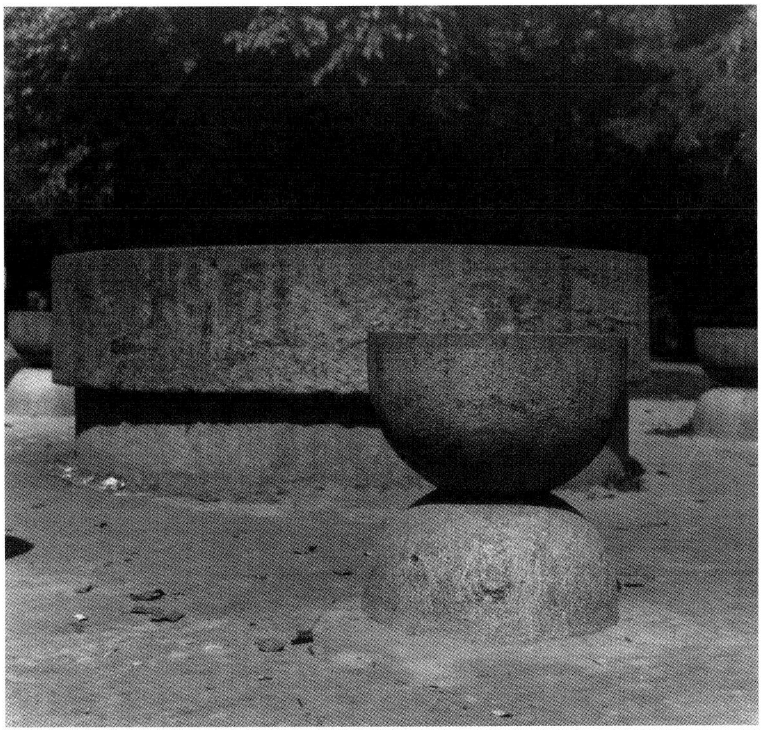

The seats surrounding the *Table of Silence* at Târgu Jiu, c.1940s

want this *Table* to be used as such, but to be *thought of* as a table, in other words to *represent* what a 'table' could mean. Once again, the works were regarded as representations of objects and not as actual objects or imitations of furniture.

Brancusi encouraged the viewer to look at his work without seeking some narrative explanation. Yet, establishing what his forms mean is difficult because he rejected any attempts to interpret them, believing that this detracted attention from the all-important task of simply looking. He wrote in the 1926 Brummer exhibition catalogue: 'Do not look for obscure formulae or for mysteries. I give you pure joy. Look at them until you see them. Those closest to God have seen them.'

How, then, are we to interpret the commission at Târgu Jiu? Like any monument, we can state that the works are site-specific; but in this case the site is also his homeland and the works represent a major achievement – the bringing home of *his* work.

Brancusi never referred to them as monuments but rather as 'my *Column*' or 'my *Gate*', adding a touch of intimacy to works that were now public. He also refused to offer any explanation that would help viewers understand the works. In a sense, this contradicts the symbolist overtones that scholars have attempted to attach to so much of his work. Whatever iconographic interpretations are put forward should be examined from the Parisian context, where Brancusi had developed so many of his ideas; for Paris provided the necessary stimulus to address, from a new perspective, his roots in Romania.

The *Column*, which from its earliest form far exceeds in scale any work of Romanian folk art, always stood alone; it was never an architectural appendage or decorative motif. If the *Column*'s shape relates in form to these

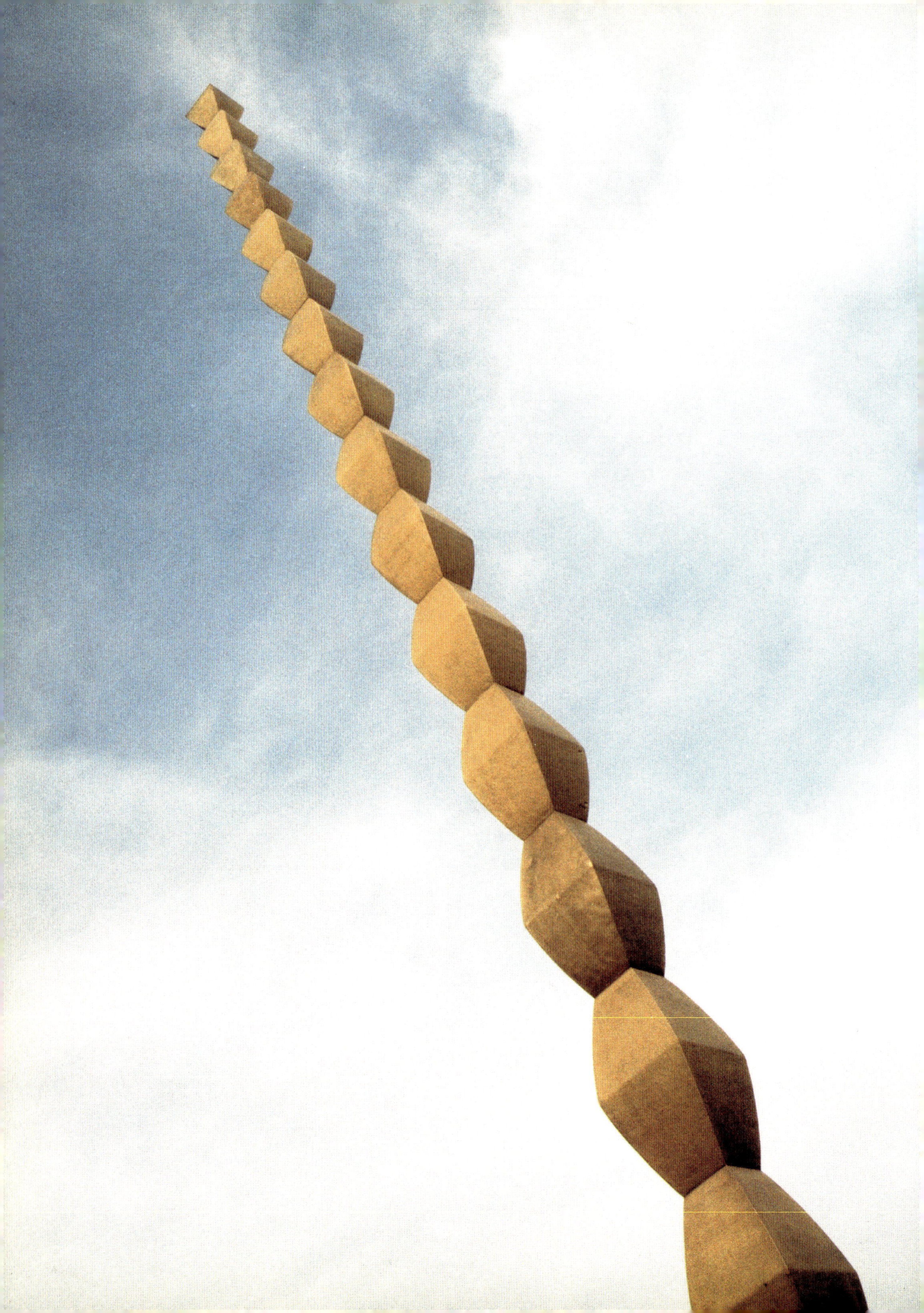

Romanian peasant motifs, its conception reaches beyond them into another cultural realm. The *Column* goes beyond the confines of folk sensibility, which is attached to the cycles of nature, and instead belongs to a sensibility that seeks to escape earthly confines and longs to be united with the infinity of space. This is a sensibility that Brancusi encountered in Paris through exposure to mystic philosophies and Buddhism.

OPPOSITE *Endless Column*, following restoration in 2000

The theme of the 'kiss' on the *Gate* has been interpreted in a way that reinforces links to Romania by asserting that it represents, metaphorically, the *Mioritsa* ballad, which describes a symbolic union with death. This narrative was deemed appropriate to a monument to fallen soldiers. But if we put aside national pride, there is another possible interpretation, one more in keeping with the image that has its roots in Brancusi's earlier funerary monument with this theme, *The Kiss* in the cemetery of Montparnasse.

In that work, the symmetrical representation of the union of two figures, male and female in perfect equanimity, has been convincingly discussed in terms of symbolist interpretations of Neoplatonic love, ideas circulating once again in Paris at the time. According to this philosophy, love is the means to attain the union between spirit and matter, and subsequently heaven and earth – a union with the celestial sphere of God, which was regarded as the ultimate end of human life. This was the interpretation that the Romanian poet Alexandru Vlahutsă (1858–1919) offered in 1910, when he discussed an earlier version of the *Kiss* (now in the Muzeul de Artà in Craiova), when it was exhibited in Bucharest.

As for the *Table*, Brancusi wanted this element to remain without a label, without anything to hold our attention except for its circular form and its position close to the ground and surrounded by 12 equidistant seats. They invite one to sit, but their distance from the *Table* precludes any functional purpose. A seated position is one of repose, and the one favoured in Far-Eastern cultures for meditation. It is the one position that Brancusi invited privileged visitors to adopt in his studio, where they would contemplate his work while resting on wooden seats.

Târgu Jiu can be regarded as a summation and synthesis of the language of Brancusi's sculpture. It was created in the intimacy of a studio, where Brancusi learned to use themes and forms as a language that was shared by a small group of friends and followers. What was once an intimate language is now in a public place, in a park that allows another kind of intimacy, one that is common to all who share the earth and sky.

The monumental ensemble of Târgu Jiu, which functions as a place of encounter, becomes, then, a place of return for Brancusi.

From Dream to Reality: Construction of the *Endless Column*

Sorana Georgescu-Gorjan

It is generally understood that artists who undertake large public projects do not work alone. More often than not, they collaborate very closely with a wide range of experts, engineers and technicians, who are crucial to completing the task and provide the necessary skills to help translate the artist's vision into reality.

That was certainly true when it came to erecting Brancusi's *Endless Column* at Târgu Jiu, which was a collaboration between the artist and many others, including the Romanian engineer Stefan Georgescu-Gorjan, and metallurgists and labourers.

From the point of view of fabrication, the *Endless Column* was the most complex component of the Târgu Jiu ensemble, and the most documented. What follows is a history of the collaborative effort between Brancusi and those in Petrosani and Târgu Jiu, who worked with him. Based on available archives, letters and other documentation, the narrative illustrates the day-to-day activities of Brancusi and Gorjan, and the steps that were often necessary to solve complex technical problems. The correspondence also describes the strong working relationship that developed between Brancusi and Gorjan, and how that bond was crucial to completing the project.

It is important to understand that the monumental ensemble was completed during a short-lived period of favourable political and cultural circumstances. That changed drastically almost immediately after the completion of the project, when World War II broke out and following that five decades of Communist dictatorship befell Romania.

Many of those who were instrumental at the time in helping to create the monument, such as Prime Minister Tatarescu, eventually became political prisoners. Tatarescu was arrested in 1950 and the valuable Tatarescu Archive was burned in the streets of Bucharest. An engineer who financed the project, Ioan Bujoiu, died in prison, while Gorjan was sentenced to years of hard labour at the Canal, the Romanian equivalent of the Gulag Archipelago. Gorjan's shorthand notebook, in which he recorded his conversations with

OPPOSITE *Endless Column* under construction, 1937, showing the tenth module being installed. View of the church in the background

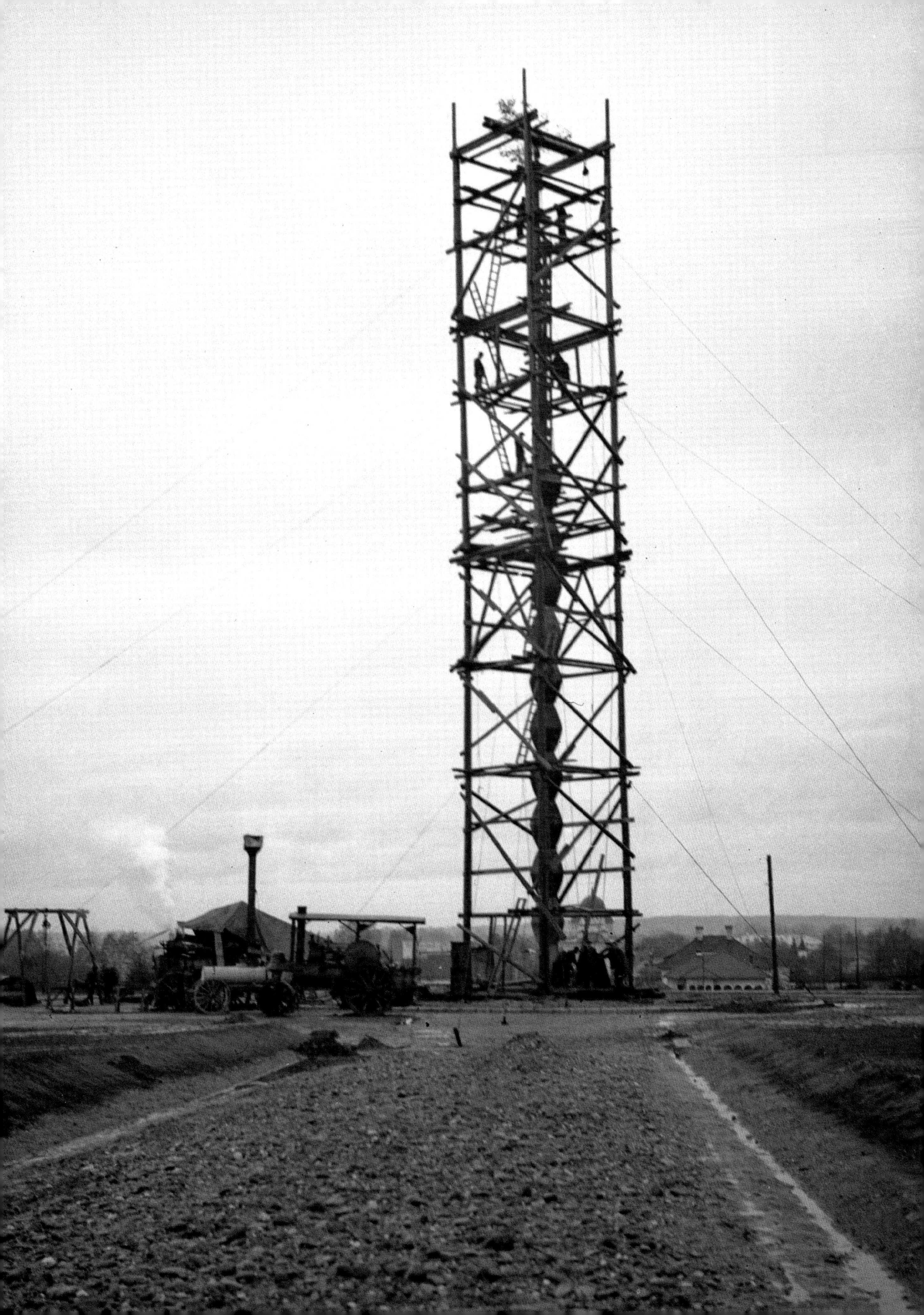

Brancusi, was lost; thankfully, though, the negatives and photos of the raising of the *Column* survived. (All the photos illustrating this essay were taken by Stefan, except for those marked 'crew photo' and the image on page 40.)

Despite his international fame, Brancusi was considered *persona non grata* by Romania's Communist regime until years after his death on 16 March 1957. As a result, his work came under suspicion and even under attack. One particularly vicious incident involving the *Column* took place during the 1950s, when local Communist authorities tried to pull down the work, which allegedly caused the *Column*'s slight deviation from the vertical.

While Gorjan carefully recorded all available data in some 40 papers published between 1964 and 1984, he failed to publish the manuscript of his book during his lifetime. Two volumes appeared posthumously: *Amintiri despre Brancusi* (Recollections on Brancusi) in 1988, and *Templul din Indor* (The Temple of Indore) in 1996. The whole text of *Am lucrat cu Brancusi* (I've Worked with Brancusi) appeared in late 2004.

THE HISTORY OF THE ENDLESS COLUMN

Brancusi had already received the invitation to build the Târgu Jiu memorial by the time Gorjan (a young engineer and the son of a close friend) visited the artist in Paris in late 1934. The sculptor had met Gorjan in 1914 and in 1922; Gorjan visited Brancusi again in Paris on 7 January 1935.

For his part, the engineer considered Brancusi a 'true artist, a genius'. So when he learned of the sculptor's intention to erect a large-scale column in Romania, Gorjan expressed interest in assisting. Gorjan's proposed solu-

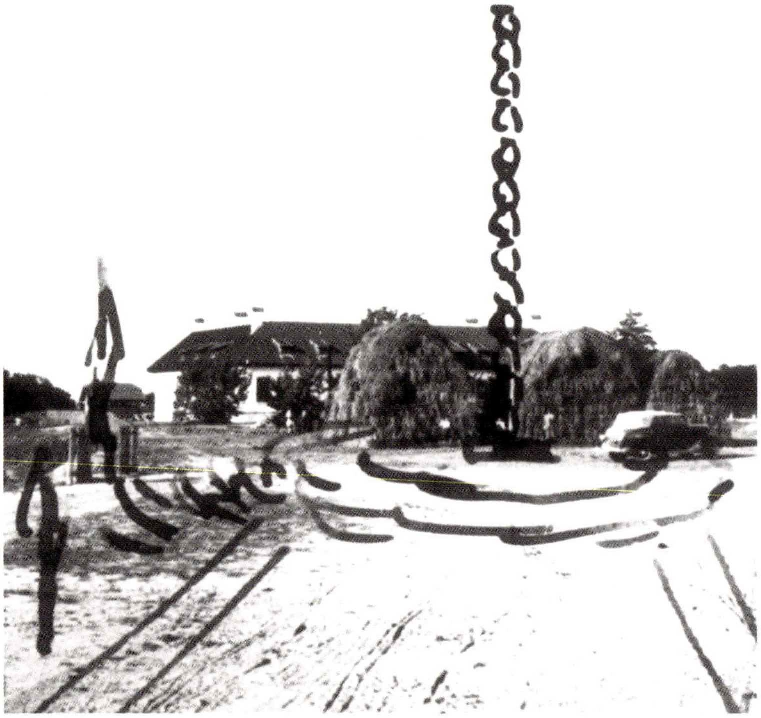

Sketch of the *Endless Column*, drawn by Brancusi on a photo of the site, 1937

tion was 'to fix the base of a solid steel pillar in a massive concrete foundation and to thread onto it giant hollow beads, the repeated identical modules of the column'. Gorjan believed that 'the perfect superposition of the modules would provide the impression of continuity'.

Gorjan, who was chief engineer at The Petrosani Central Workshops, accepted Brancusi's request for assistance with technical matters. The Petrosani company, which specialized in mining, was the most important of its kind in Romania. Its director general, Ioan Bujoiu, was also minister of industry and commerce in the Tatarescu cabinet in 1937, and in that capacity, earmarked more than two million Lei for the project. Tatarescu agreed that Gorjan should coordinate the technical aspects of the project inside Petrosani.

During 1936 and 1937, there were several more meetings in Paris between Brancusi and Gorjan. The sculptor specified that cast iron was to be used for the modules, which he also called 'elements' or 'beads'. Brancusi considered this metal to be the most enduring; furthermore, it could be coated with a golden-yellow layer by spraying on brass.

Brancusi arrived in Romania in June 1937 to study possible sites in Târgu Jiu, and made three preliminary choices for the ensemble: the *Table* would be on the banks of the River Jiu and close to the bridge where an important World War I battle took place; the *Gate* at the entrance to the public park; and the *Column* on the so-called 'Hay Market' grounds to the east end of Târgu Jiu. During June and July, he supervised stonecutters from the city of Deva who roughed the travertine blocks for the *Gate of the Kiss*. This work was based on a plaster model that Brancusi had cast in 1935.

In late July, Brancusi walked with Gorjan from the banks of the Jiu, through the public park and to the site selected for the *Column*. Gorjan took a photo of the site, with the haystacks in the background. On this snapshot, Brancusi drew the sketch of a column, resembling the oil-press screw in his Paris studio. Using Gorjan's fountain pen, which produced a thick line in blue ink, Brancusi produced a drawing that shows a lawn around the column, a circular path, radial walks and several poplar trees (opposite).

In the first half of August, at the Petrosani factory, Brancusi and Gorjan finalized the basic proportions for the module. Brancusi wanted the total height of a module to be four times the side of the narrow base and twice that of the central width. The range of technical issues had to be reconciled with the budget, which was exceeded in the end.

Gorjan, assisted by another engineer at Petrosani, Nicolae Hasnas, made a rough estimate of the costs. Brancusi and Gorjan, working in the engineer's house, arrived at a first method for a 20-metre-high column with 12 full modules and a small side of 37.5 centimetres. Alternative proposals included a 15-module column. Eventually, Brancusi decided on a 15-module column, with a small side of 45 centimetres and total height of 29.35 metres.

The actual work began in mid-August 1937, when carpenters made a rough 45 x 90 x 180 centimetre softwood model (right); Brancusi personally finished one side of the model until the desired curvature was obtained. The other three sides were finished to match by the master carpenter Carol

Rough softwood model of a module before carving

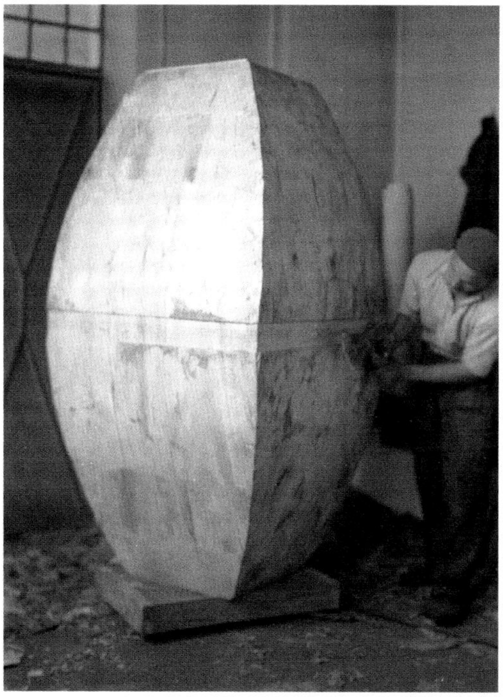

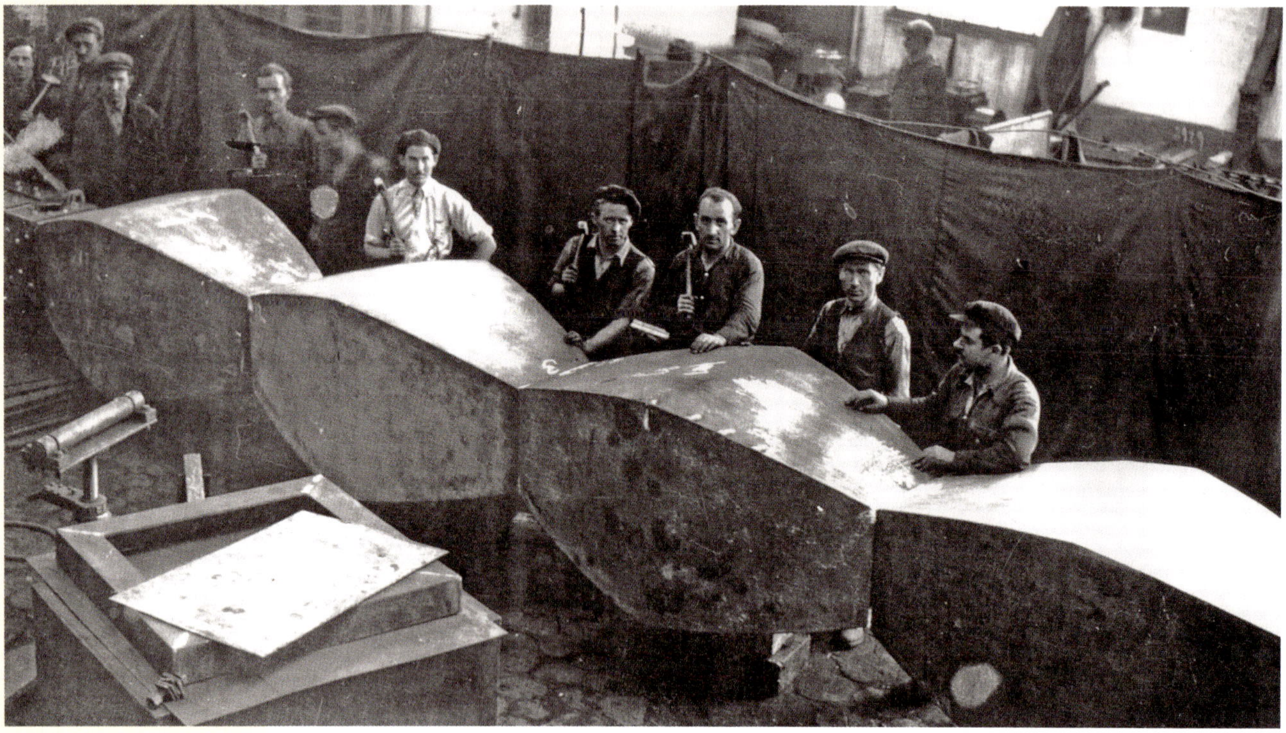

Test assembly in the shop

Fliszek. Red lacquer was applied on the surface of the wood prototype, and the core box, armature and special frame were fabricated. Brancusi, who considered himself a craftsman, worked with the carpenters in the factory's model shop. Unfortunately, the model carved by Brancusi has been lost, but documents and sketches relating to it are preserved in the company archive.

In August, Gorjan ordered rolled steel and plates from the Resita steel mill and Malaxa Works in Bucharest. Production was then expedited following the direct intervention of the Romanian prime minister, and the foundry model was completed on 1 September, the date that appears on plan AP 2150 of the spine.

By this time, though, Brancusi had returned to France. On 2 September, he wrote a letter 'from the train', telling Gorjan that he could no longer stop to see the model, but that he expected it would be satisfactory. The artist requested speedy completion of the foundation, and asked to be informed when the 'elements' were to be cast. He also noted that Aretie Tatarescu (the prime minister's wife) had expressed the desire that the cast iron should not be finished with a smooth surface. However, Gorjan mentions that the final versions of the surfaces were actually smooth, and that the sculptor was pleased with them. The foundation could not be completed before the fabrication of the steel spine; the excavation began on 15 September 1937.

In the Metal Structures Department, the steel spine was fabricated by a crew headed by an experienced foreman Ioan Romosan. The master welder Victor Borodi used electric welding. The steel spine of the *Column* was designed in three sections to allow transportation along the winding Jiu mountain pass, from Petrosani to Târgu Jiu. The sections are 8.93 metres, 10 metres and 9.4 metres long, which total 28.33 metres. A special structure –

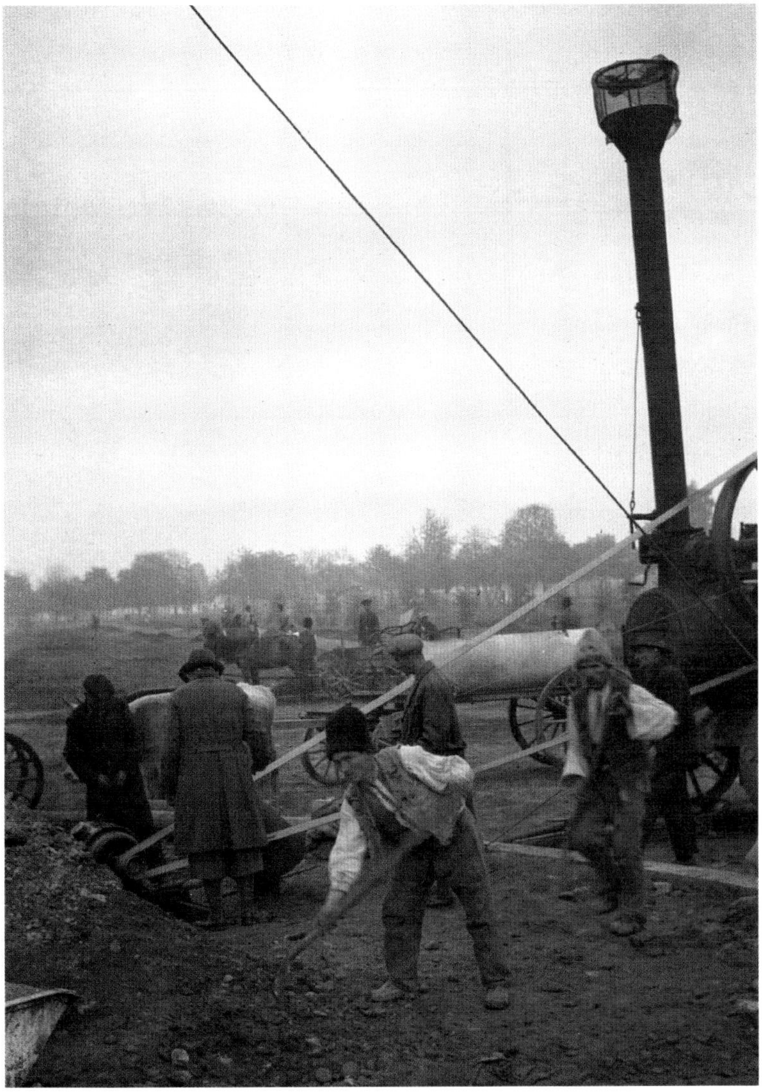

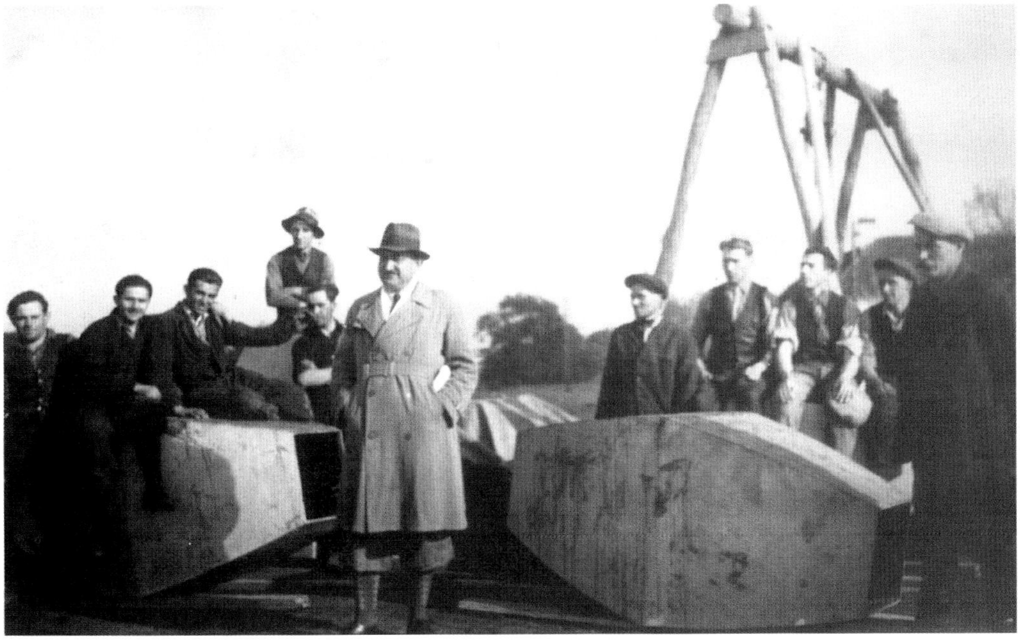

ABOVE The work site is being organized

LEFT The unloaded modules on site (crew photo)

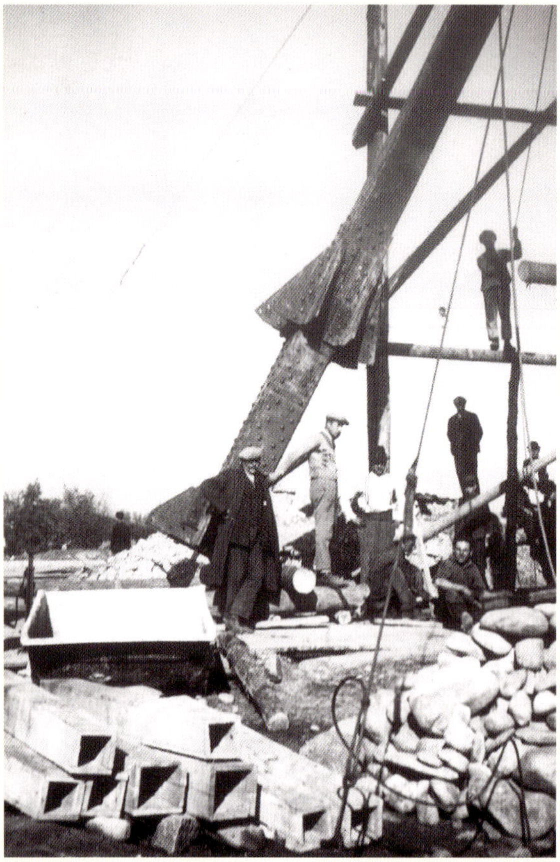

LEFT The raising of the cross-trestle structure (crew photo)

BELOW The unloading of the tools

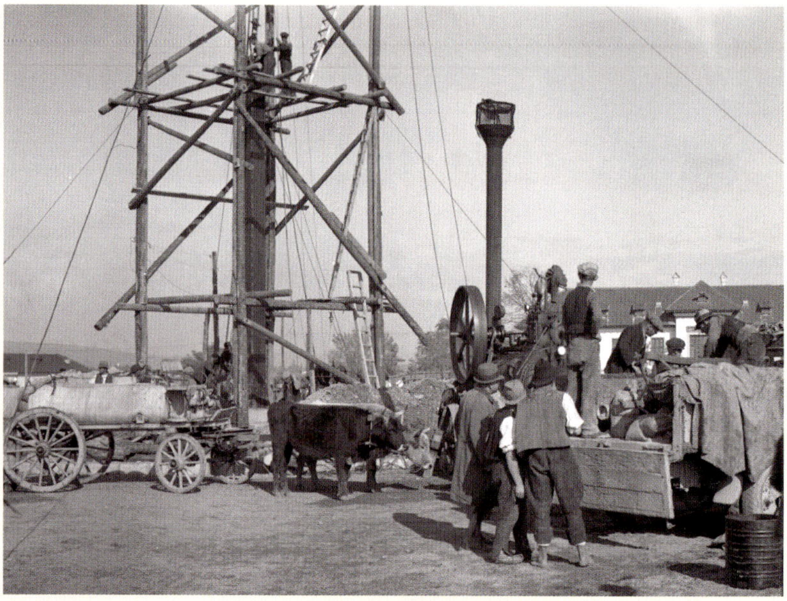

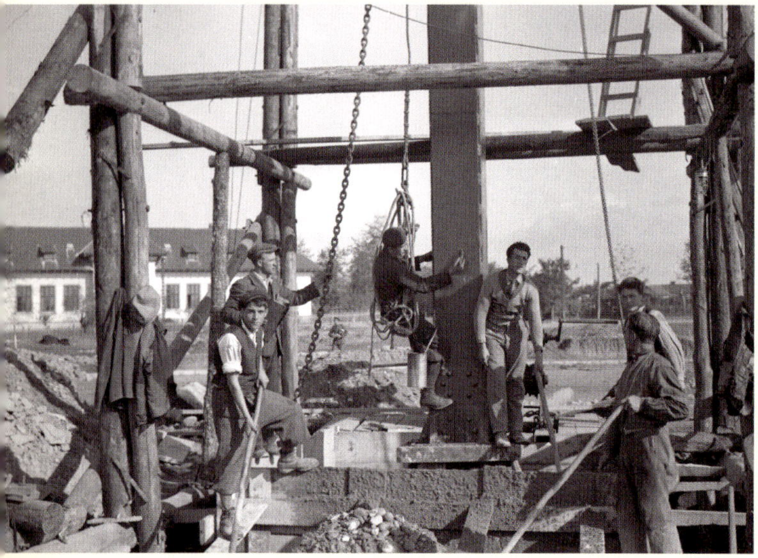

ABOVE The painting of the structural core

RIGHT The installation of the lower half-module

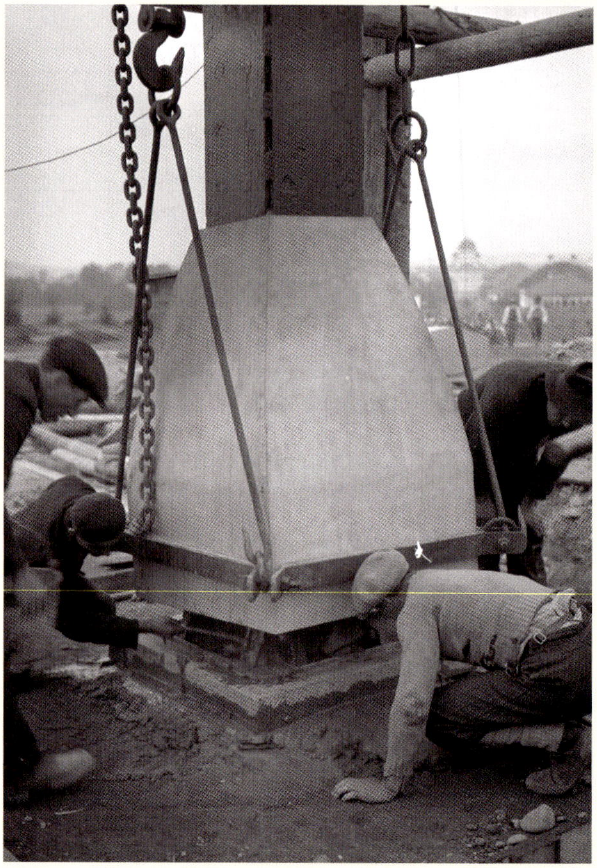

a three-metre-long 'cross-trestle' – was embedded in the concrete foundation to support the *Column*. To protect the project's steel core against corrosion, two coats of red lead primer were applied on the sections in the workshop; a third layer was added later, on site.

In answer to Gorjan's letters of 3 and 16 September, Brancusi cabled from Paris, on 20 September, to say that, 'metallization has to be yellow. Have you cast any elements?' Metallization tests performed in the shop used brass wire with an alloy that darkened easily. Cast modules were sanded with a special device, coated with a zinc layer and then plated with brass. The Petrosani foundry finished module casting in October; ten were completed by 12 October, and three others were cast on 18 October.

Brancusi was informed by Gorjan that the excavation of the foundation at Târgu Jiu was difficult due to heavy rains. The foundation was shaped like a truncated stepped pyramid, five metres below grade, with a base four-and-a-half-metres square, into which 75 cubic metres of concrete weighing 165 tons were poured. Brancusi's letter of 15 October 1937 to Gorjan said the artist could not return to Romania as promised, but hoped to arrive on 26 October. He urged a yellow metallization for the modules and the use of high-quality concrete for the foundation.

Gorjan's letter of 18 October to Brancusi discussed problems related to the module casting, such as how the plane parallel surfaces of the modules were carefully machined to ensure a perfect fit. Gorjan also described the difficulties encountered in transporting the lower-spine section (weighing over nine tons) on an iron carriage pulled by caterpillar vehicles and escorted by two trucks. The carriage and one truck broke down; the entire operation lasted three days and included an escort squad of volunteer firemen.

The test assembly of the *Column* was performed in the shop in October, and order numbers were punched on modules, to ensure accurate on-site assembly. Gorjan photographed the operation (page 34). Gorjan's and others' photographs during the raising of the *Column* provide an almost cinematic documentary of the work involved. One image shows horse- and ox-driven carts from which gravel is unloaded, an ox-driven tank bringing water and mechanics coupling an electric engine with a belt (page 35, top).

One photo (page 35, bottom), taken by a mechanic, shows the crew close to the unloaded cast-iron modules. A wooden portal with a hand-operated hoisting block is used to unload the modules from the truck. Francisc Hering, the head of the mounting operation, stands on the right, with a white cap and moustache. Other photos taken by workers illustrate the hoisting of the cross-trestle structure to be embedded in the foundation (opposite: top left).

A photo, taken by Gorjan, shows how the tools and materials were unloaded from a truck. A waterproof tarpaulin, visible on its side, was used to protect modules during transportation. For security reasons, modules were brought from Petrosani, only when their turn came for 'threading'. The lower-spine section, already joined to the embedded structure, and the scaffolding can be observed in the background (opposite: top right).

The last concrete layer is then poured on the upper part of the founda-

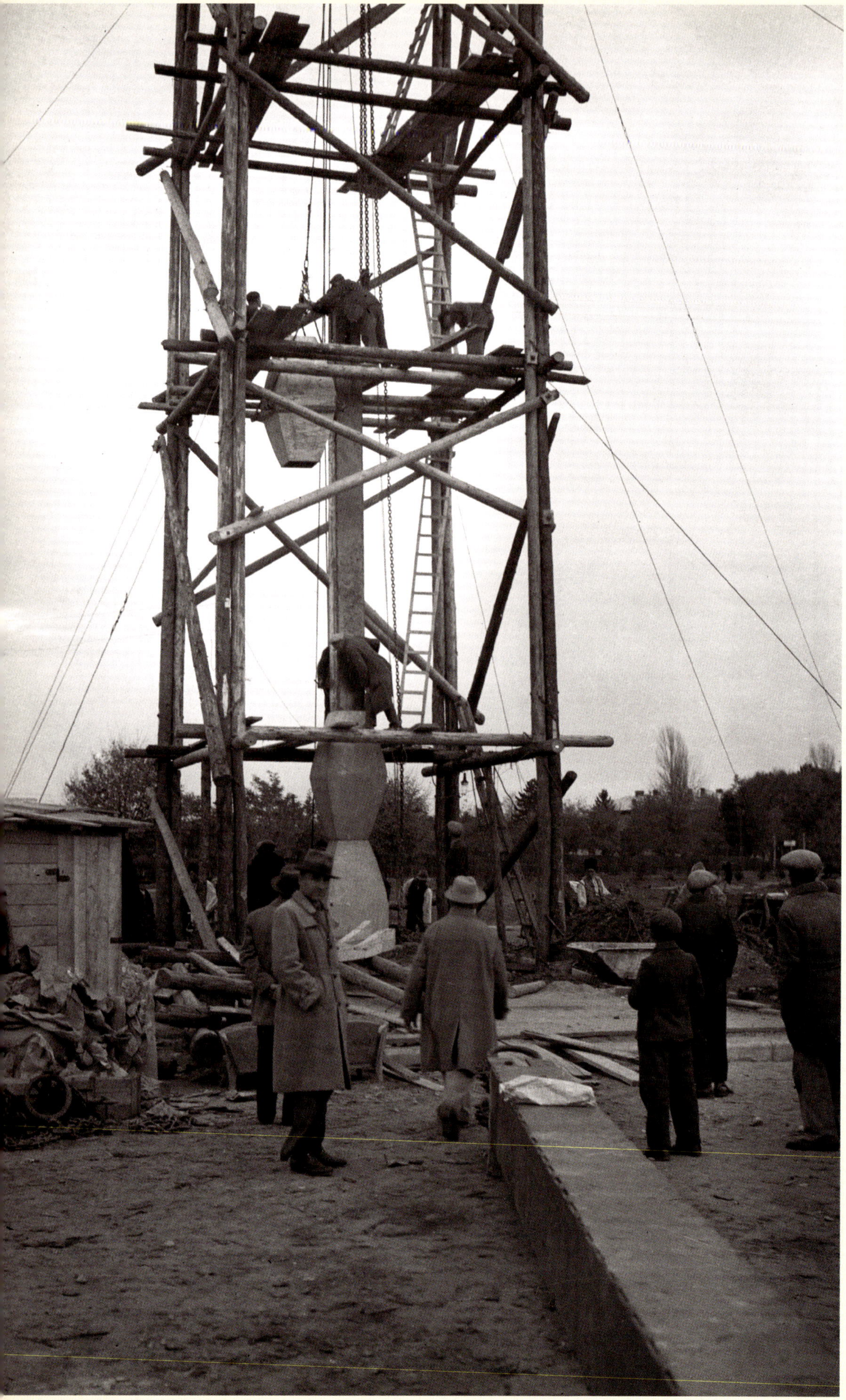

LEFT Brancusi goes to the scaffolding. The hoisting of module II

OPPOSITE:

TOP LEFT Brancusi supervises the operations. Threading of module II

TOP RIGHT The raising of the middle-spine section

BOTTOM LEFT Structural detail of the upper-spine section

BOTTOM RIGHT The assembly crew (crew photo)

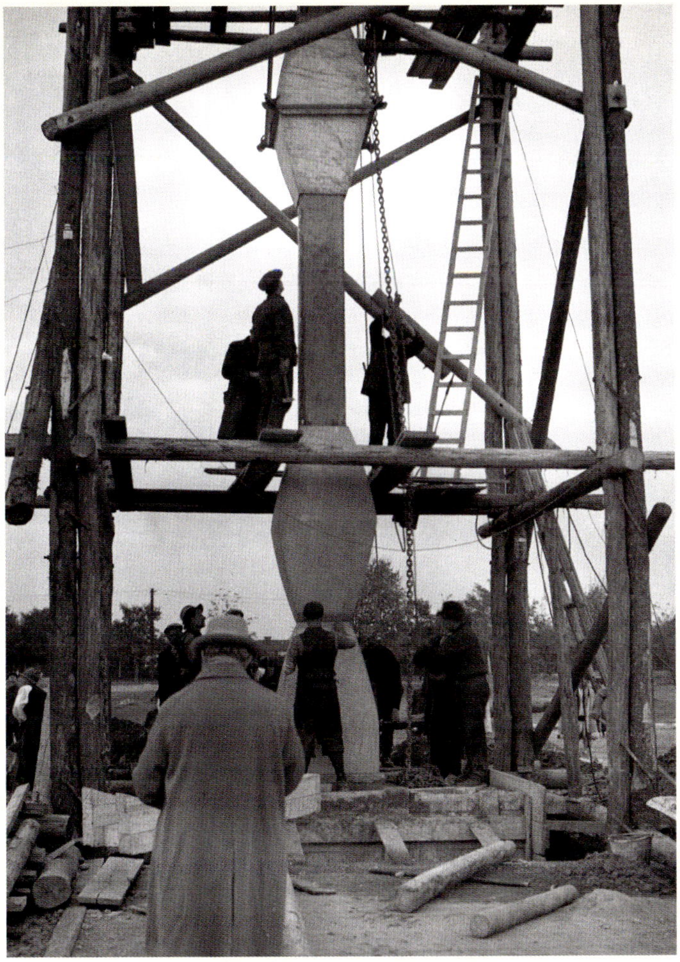
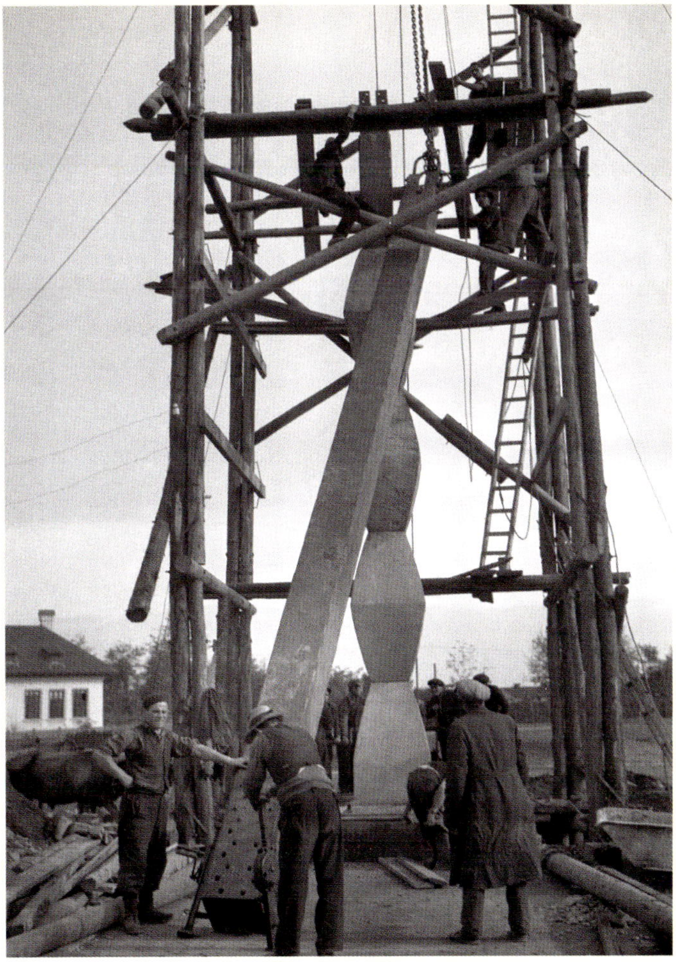
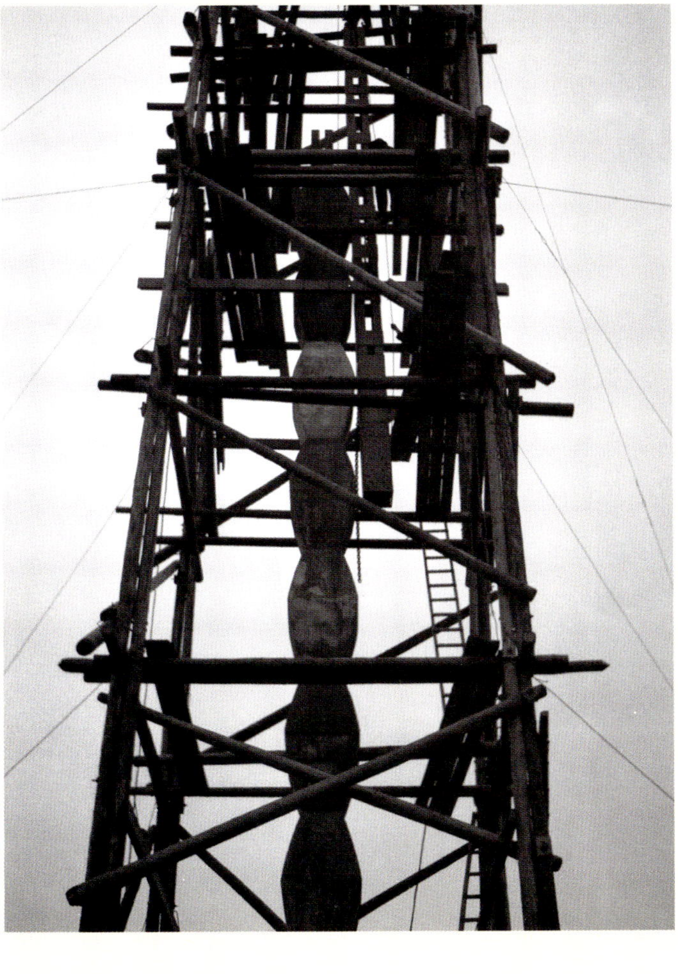
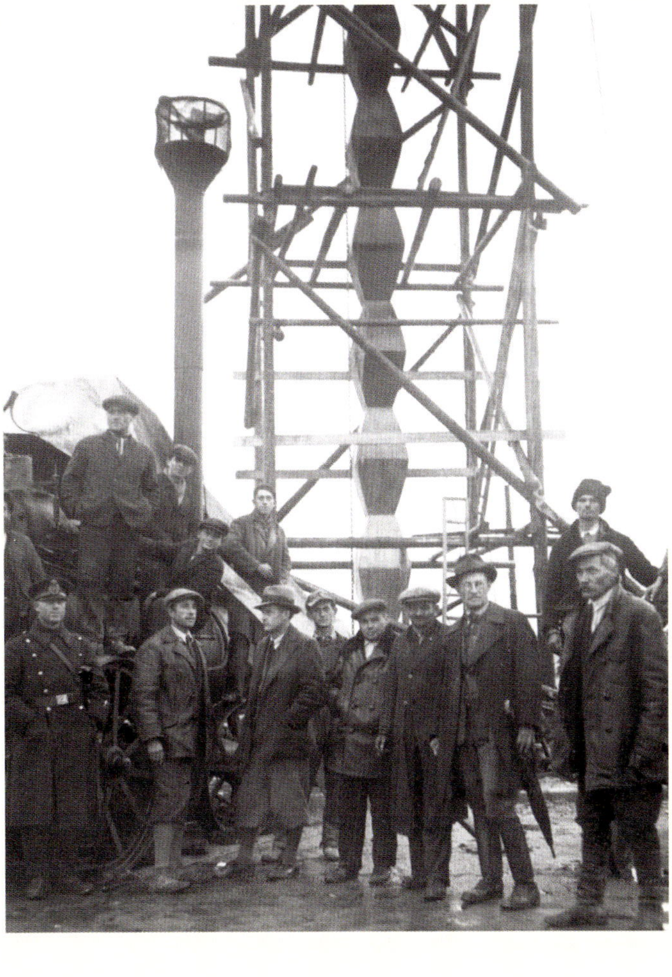

Endless Column at Târgu Jiu, 1938, photogram. Constantin Brancusi Bequest, 1957. Musée national d'art moderne, Centre Pompidou, Paris

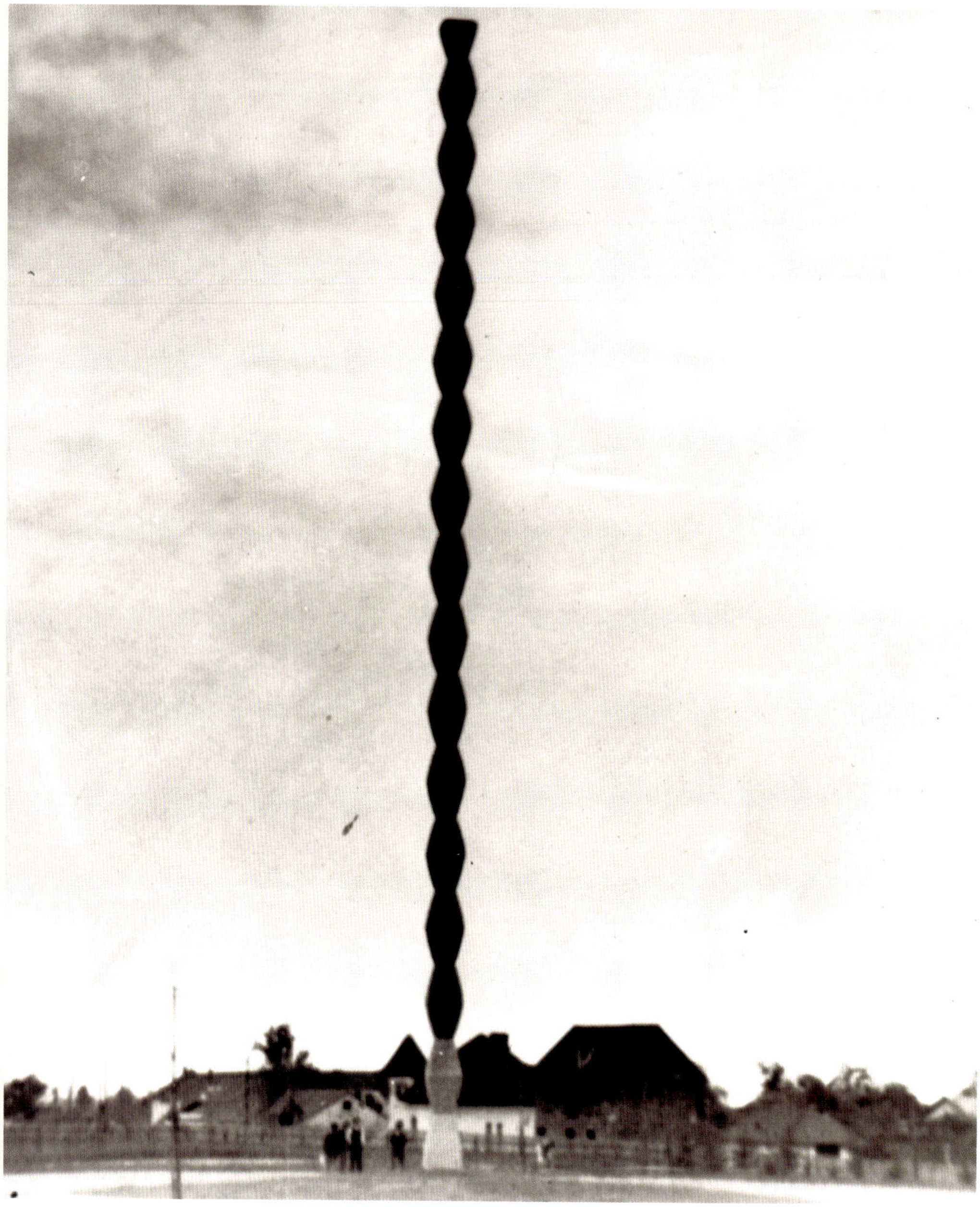

tion. The upper portion (page 36, bottom left) of the 'cross-trestle' fins – supporting a steel frame, standing on welded steel strips – is also visible. Foreman Perini leans against the spine. Iosif Moldovan, suspended in a 'swing', applies the last layer of red lead primer on the spine. Iosif Demeter, Francisc Gundel and Ioan Perdi are also present. Discontinued welding seams and the riveting of the fins are clearly seen. The bottom-most half-module with its 45-centimetre prismatic base is then placed on the steel frame (page 36, bottom right). The fins of the cross-trestle helped to firmly fix the *Column*'s base and an ingenious device was used to thread the module (a collarband bolted to it, four rings and two pairs of rigid rods).

In late October, Brancusi came to Târgu Jiu to inspect the roughly made *Gate*, the cleared allée in the park and the first version of the *Table*, close to the dam. He attended the dedication of the Church of the Apostles Peter and Paul on 7 November. At the site of the *Column*, Brancusi personally supervised the threading down of the first full modules. Photos taken by Gorjan in November include two views of Brancusi with his back towards the camera (the artist did not enjoy being photographed by others). In one (page 38), Brancusi is walking towards the *Column* to have a look at the gripping device and hoisting block. In another (page 39, top left) he is shown standing close to the scaffolding as module II is being threaded down on the spine.

Satisfied with the way operations were proceeding, Brancusi entrusted Gorjan with supervising the remaining work, as the artist was expected in India to take on a commission by the Maharajah of Indore to build a temple. (The project was eventually abandoned.) On the site, module III was threaded on the spine and then the middle-spine section was hoisted with a pulley and a jack, and welded together with the lower section. An anti-rust layer was applied on that section; the hoisting of the middle spine section is shown on page 39, top right.

The photo on page 39, bottom left, shows shows a clear image of the latticework used in the upper-spine section. Another (page 31) provides a general view of the *Column* with ten modules threaded down. The outline of the church on the Avenue of the Heroes is visible in the background. The last photo taken by the assembly crew (page 39, bottom right) shows them close to the *Column* (foreman Hering on the right and foreman Perini on the left). The operation was completed without accidents.

The *Column* was completed by the middle of November 1937, although the scaffolding was maintained for the metallization to be completed the following year. Brancusi returned to Romania in June 1938, and he finished the *Gate of the Kiss* around mid-July, with the assistance of the stonemason Ion Alexandrescu. Brancusi ordered a second table in August. He made a new table from the upper stone slabs of the former two, and then placed it on the site selected as early as 1937. The stone stools surrounding the *Table* and the square stools for the 'Allée of Stools' were placed in early September.

The modules were sprayed on site, first with zinc and then with brass by the Metalizarea Company of Bucharest, between 20 June and 25 July 1938. According to Gorjan, Brancusi was satisfied by tests that used a high-purity brass alloy. Fragments of Brancusi's correspondence do mention bronze; yet this involves a period prior to the final decision. The Istrati–Dumitrescu Archive, recently made available to the public, may illuminate many other questions still left unanswered, including whether Brancusi was present at the dedication of the memorial on 27 October 1938. Gorjan was travelling abroad on that date.

For decades after completion of the *Column*, Gorjan was concerned with its preservation, and was involved in a succession of restoration projects: in 1965–66, 1975–76 and 1983–84. He died on 5 March 1985. After 1989, following the fall of the Communist regime, there were new initiatives to restore the *Column*. Some said it should be coated with gold; others believed that it was about to topple over. Eventually, the *Column* was restored according to Brancusi's documented intentions.

Restoration of the *Endless Column*, *Table of Silence* and *Gate of the Kiss*

Mihai Radu

At its best, public art has the capacity to create and enhance urban spaces. In creating the monumental ensemble, Brancusi thought that even a small nondescript town plaza such as that in Târgu Jiu could be transformed through a judicious use of art to create a new sense of 'urbanism'. For the artist, the ensemble, far from being mere urban furniture disguised as art, offered the potential to transform a provincial context into a modern concept, with long-lasting planning implications.

Unfortunately, Brancusi's vision for the ensemble had yet to be fully realized when the first signs of deterioration became evident, just a quarter of a century after the monument's construction. Weather and time had taken their toll, particularly on the plated cast-iron modules of the *Column*. Exposure to the elements had resulted in severe surface deterioration and discoloration – damage that, according to local reports, may have been compounded by an attempt by the Communist authorities to dismantle the *Column* at some point during the 1950s.

Prior to the recent restoration campaign, the *Column* had been re-plated three times: 1965–66, 1975–76 and 1983–84. Prior restorations focused only on the *Column's* exterior, ignoring the condition of the spine. This work helped to protect the modules' exterior from further deterioration, but did little to stop the deterioration of the spine or inner surface of the modules.

From 1984 until 1996, all the monuments were left untouched; the condition of the spine and module surface of the *Endless Column* was gradually deteriorating. The two travertine monuments located in the Municipal Park at the opposite end of the town – the *Table of Silence* and *Gate of the Kiss* – were even more unfortunate in their neglect, as they had not been restored since their completion in 1938. The Avenue of the Heroes, which connects the two parks, suffered even more adverse transformations. During the 1980s, it changed from a quaint sleepy street into an overly developed residential and commercial strip, which was a direct result of megalomaniacal urban concepts, dictated by the Communist regime as a national reconstruction project. All these factors and the precarious conditions of the ensemble

OPPOSITE Module XIII stripped of the old metal plating and waiting in preparation for the metal coating, 2000

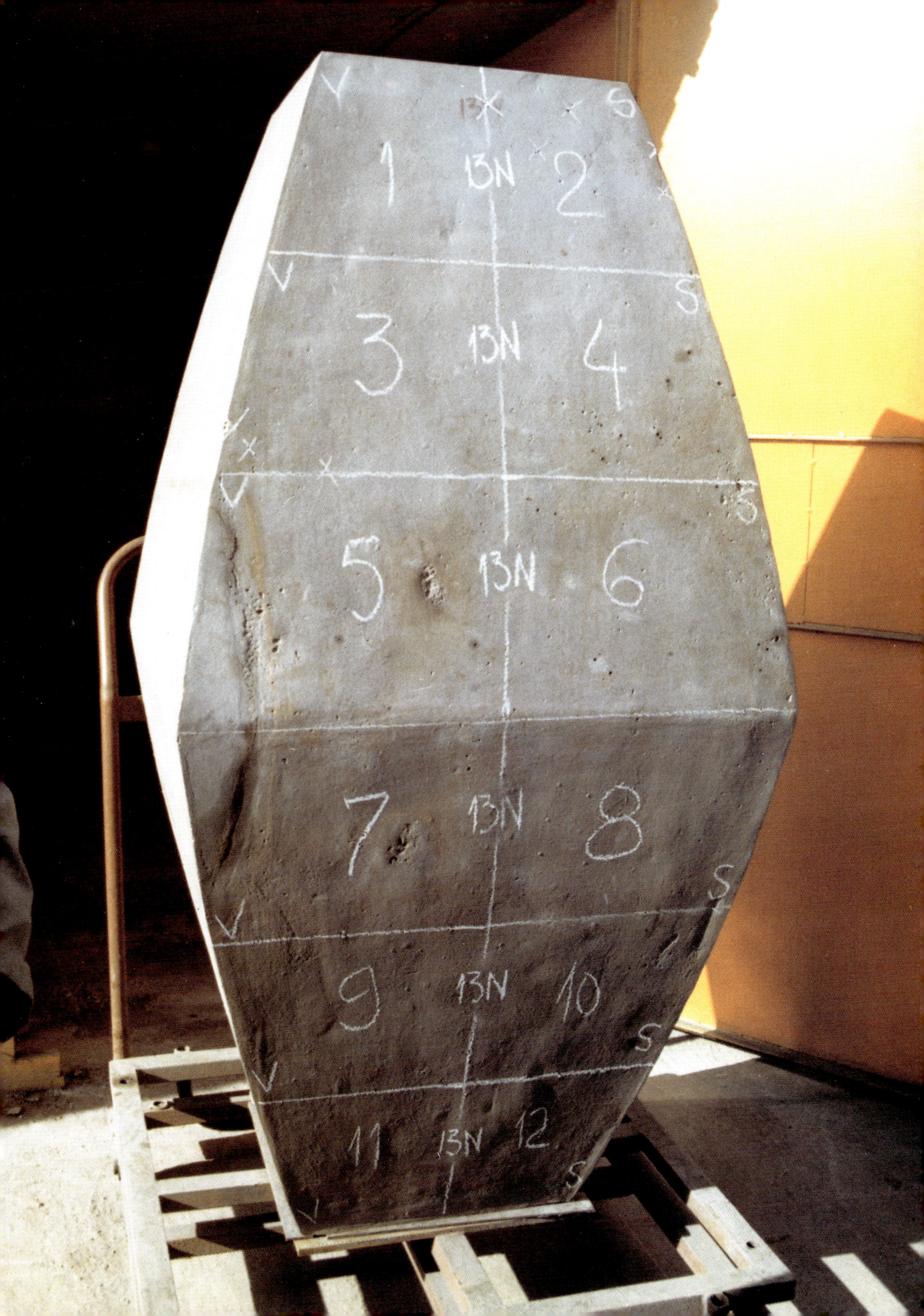
V
S
1
13N
2
V
S
3
13N
4
V
5
13N
6
7
13N
8
S
V
9
13N
10
S
V
11
13N
12
S
V

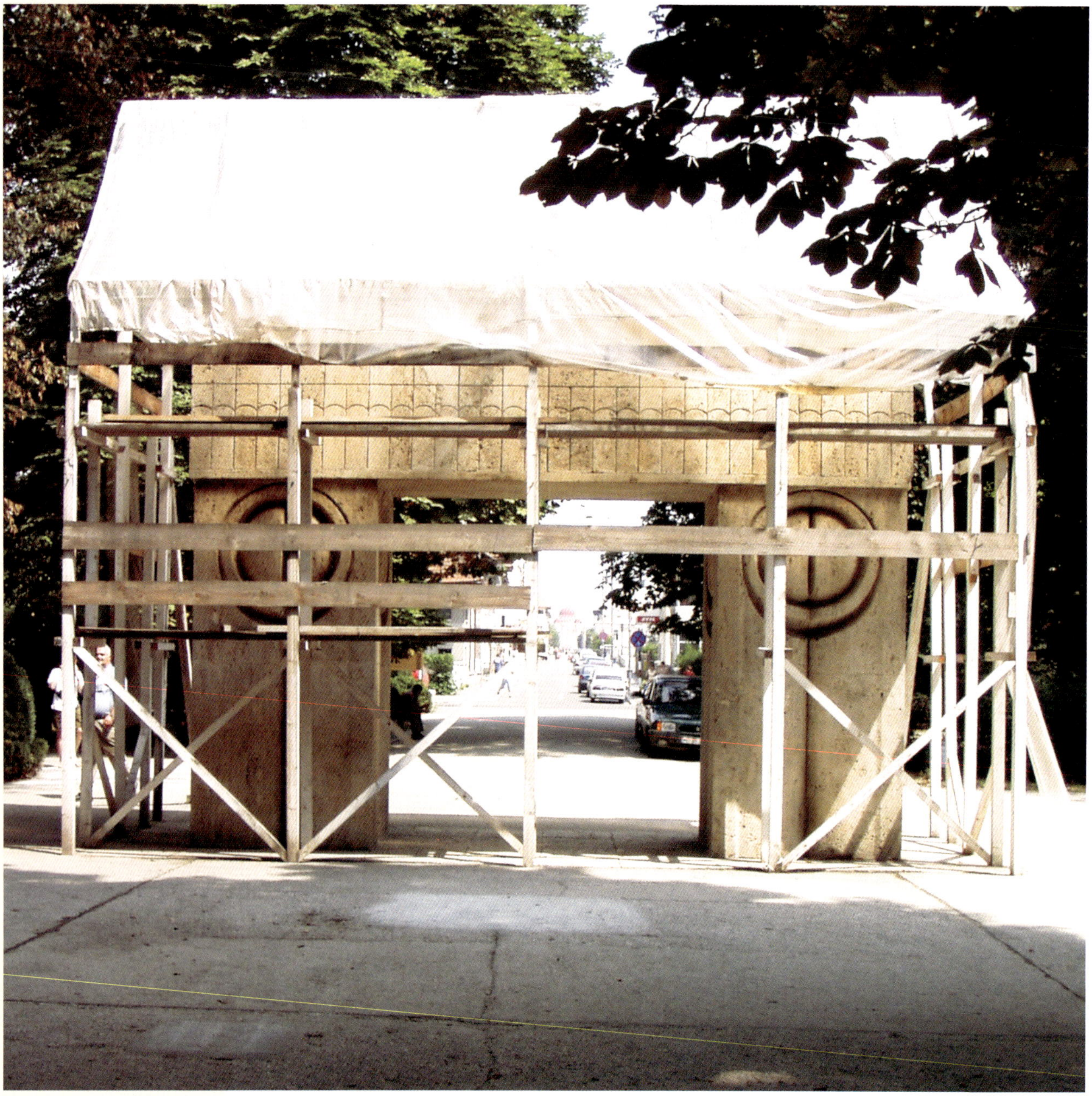

The protection tent over the *Gate of the Kiss* during restoration in 2000

convinced WMF to include it on their Watch® list in 1996 as an endangered site.

Brancusi's ideas about the urban fabric of a city involved making small-scale interventions connected by an overall idea about the structure and life of a contemporary city. His position was a radical one relative to urban design dogma of the mid-twentieth century, which seemed to assume that only large-scale interventions were consequential. A key example of such an unfortunate large-scale intervention is the destruction of a substantial portion of Bucharest's centre during the Ceausescu period, which was done to create space for the megalomaniacal palace – the Casa Poporului – for the leader and his associates.

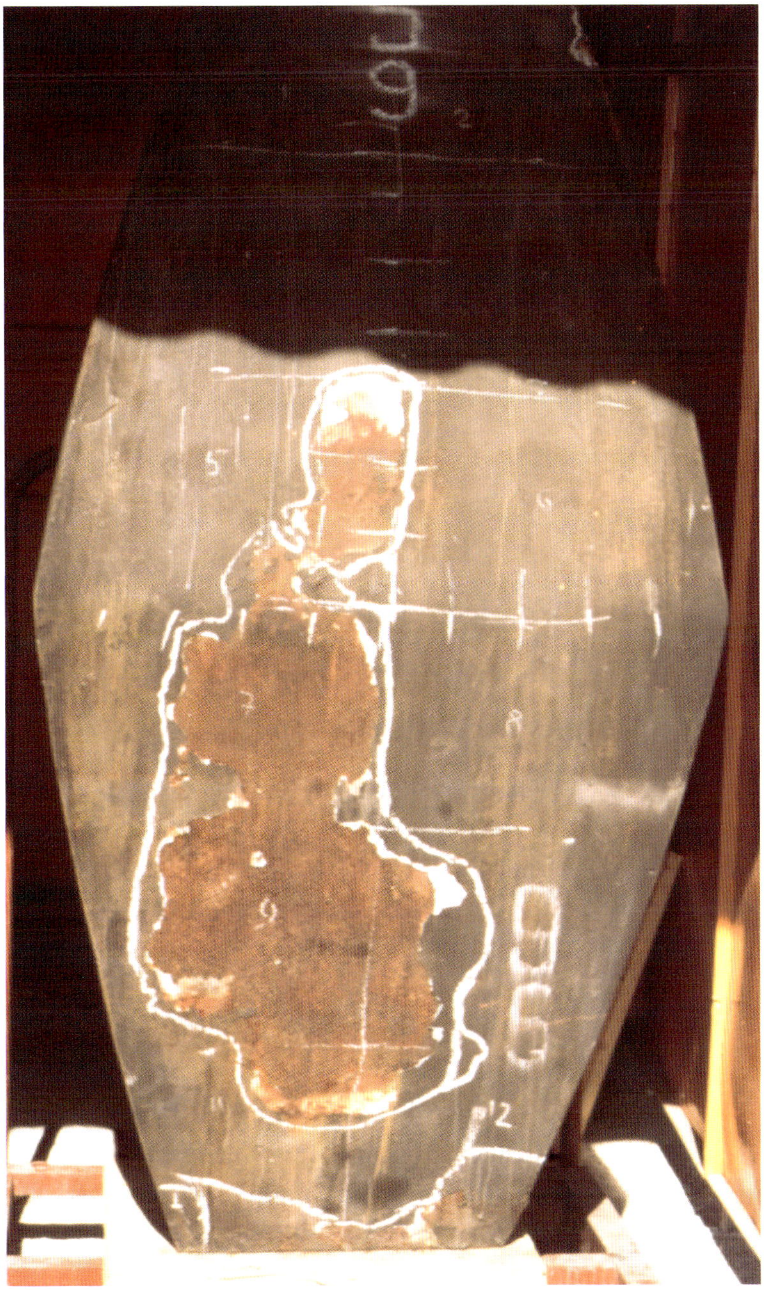

LEFT The extent of the surface corrosion of one of the *Endless Column* modules is visible

BELOW Significant corrosion is visible at the base of the *Column*

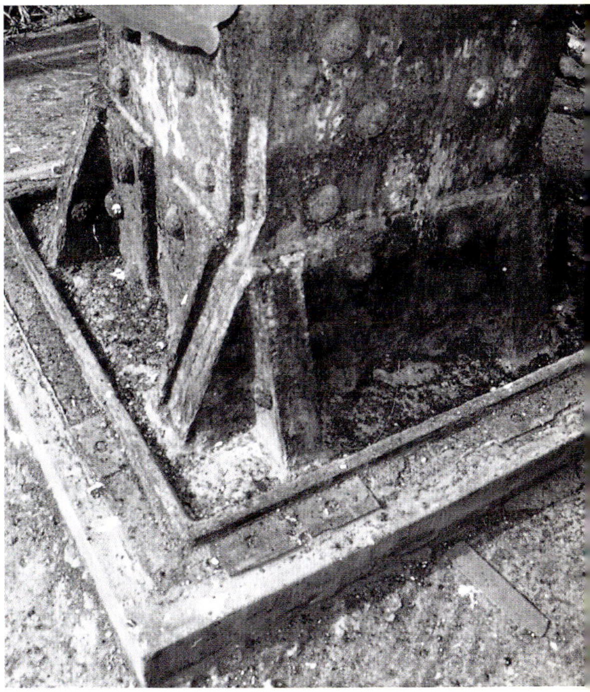

By the end of Ceausescu's regime in 1989, Târgu Jiu's town centre and the Avenue of the Heroes had been overwhelmed by the new, over-developed administrative and commercial centre, and a series of uninspiring, oversized residential buildings. As is typical of its kind, Romania's Communist regime attempted to recast Târgu Jiu in its own image, demolishing buildings and city centres in the hope of erasing the past and allowing a 'new egalitarian reality' to emerge. Equally typical and tragic, the leadership further justified its 'interventions' in Târgu Jiu by labelling Brancusi's art 'decadent' – the ultimate condemnation in that cultural climate. Had their efforts been more effective, the half-hearted demolition attempt on the *Column* in the 1950s might have succeeded, at a tremendous loss to the art world.

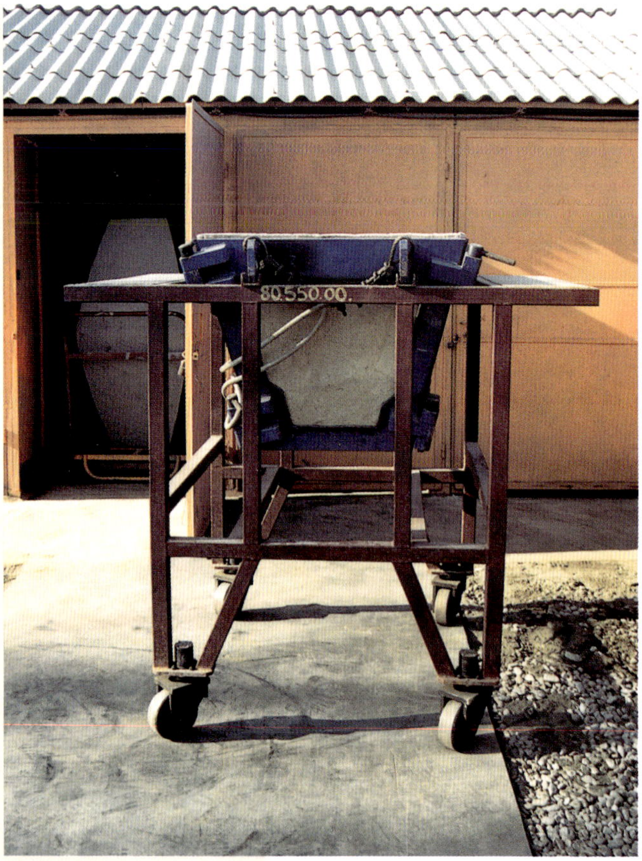

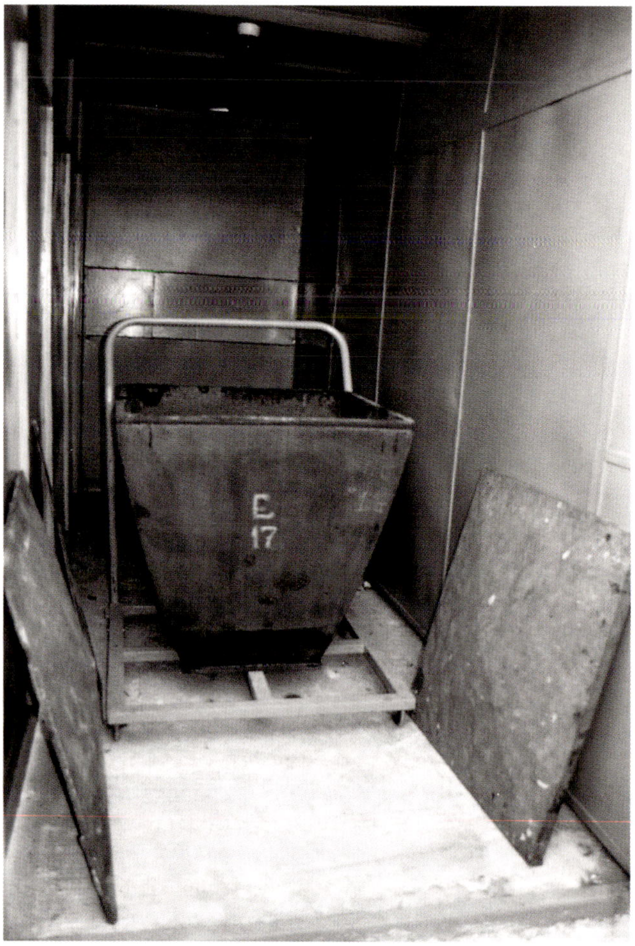

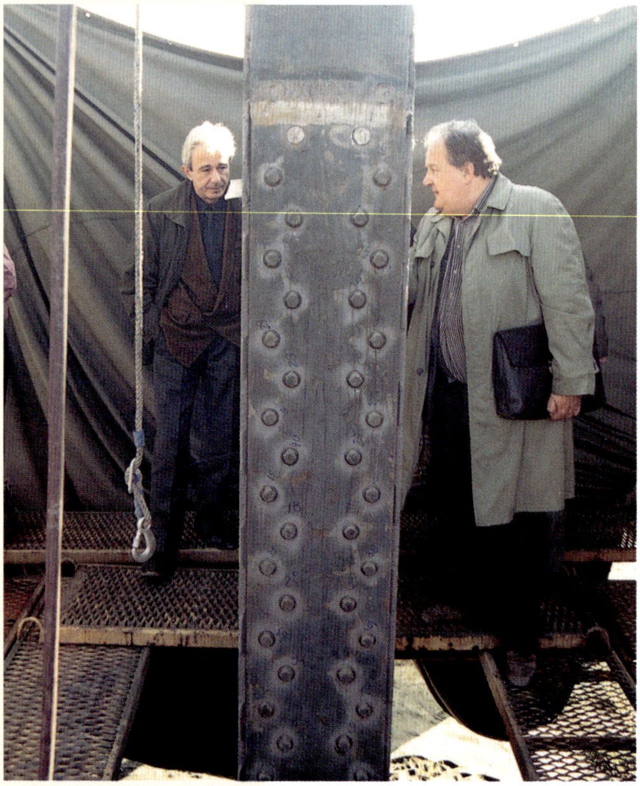

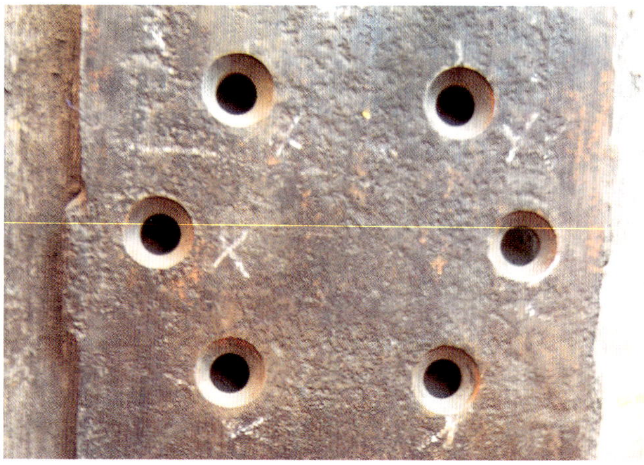

CLOCKWISE FROM TOP LEFT Transportation cradle for the *Column* modules; the storage units for the *Column* modules; an example of the spine metal plate; structural engineering consultants inspecting the replacement metal plate at the base of the spine after installation

OPPOSITE Final metal plating of the *Column* modules

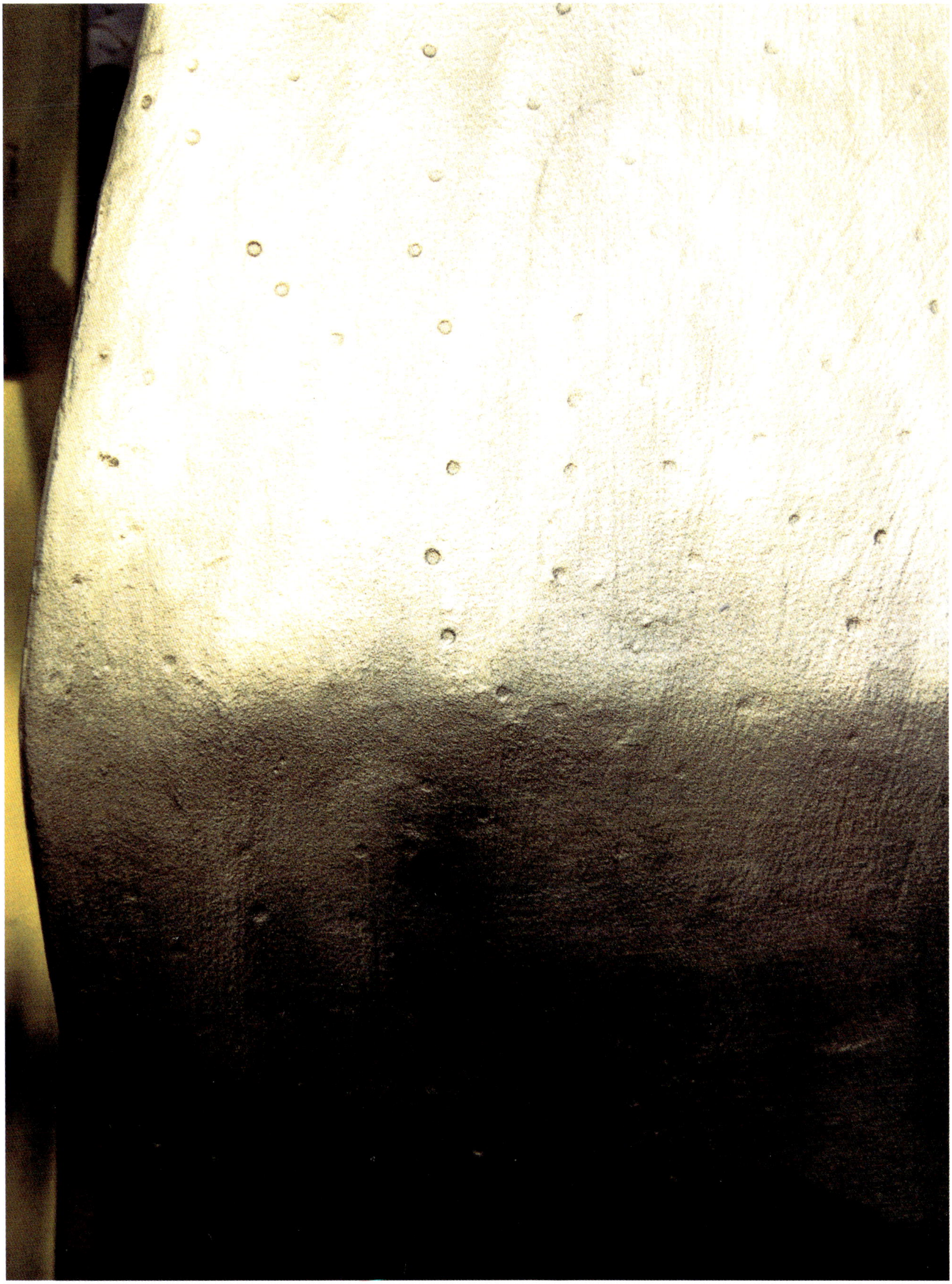

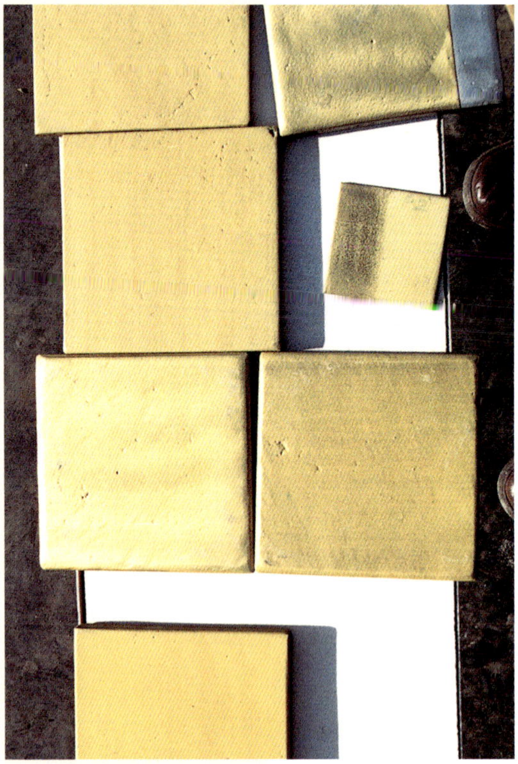

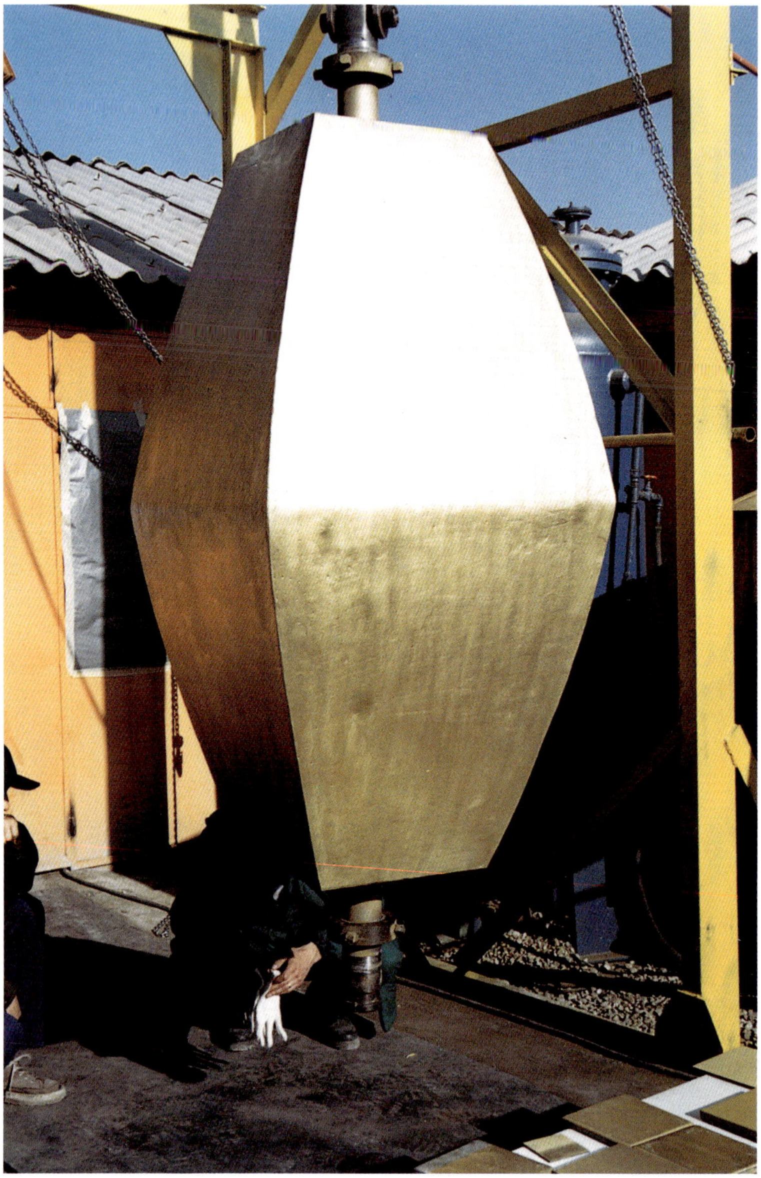

ABOVE Metal plating samples

RIGHT One of the modules being prepared for the final hand-polishing phase

By the time of its inclusion on WMF's 1996 list of *100 Most Endangered Sites*, the *Column* had been disassembled by a local group founded by the Romanian art world figure, Radu Varia, with approval of the Romanian authorities. In preparation for yet a fourth re-plating, its modules were placed in storage while its steel spine was left unprotected, exposed to the region's rain and heavy snow. The group had no resources to complete the project; the management of the project was eventually shifted to the Ministry of Culture, joined by WMF and the World Bank.

Much like Brancusi's work on the ensemble itself, our efforts to preserve the site began with the *Endless Column* alone – a targeted effort to conserve and restore the monument's most prominent element. Only later did it expand to incorporate the other sculptural elements – the *Table of Silence* and *Gate of the Kiss*.

As the project evolved, however, we saw the potential to fully realize

Brancusi's visionary blend of art and urban design as an integral part of the city. Carried to completion, the restoration of the whole of the ensemble and its landscape could serve as a catalyst for the revitalization of Târgu Jiu.

In 1997, the WMF brought together an international team of preservation professionals, who arrived on site to assess the scope of work necessary for its restoration. As a first step, the team of specialists ensured that the existing storage facilities were adequate for the protection of the modules during the restoration period. Solutions for the protection of the spine were also discussed and soon after, the spine protection was implemented. Tight security and other protocols were also imposed to make sure no modules were lost or damaged.

The project team then devised a strategy to address each of the project components – restoration of the sculptural elements; development of the master plan for Târgu Jiu, which included urban planning and the design of a new visitor centre; and landscaping of the site to re-establish its sanctity while integrating it into its urban environment. The latter would be carried out by the Olin Partnership, a Philadelphia-based landscape design company (see next chapter), in association with Romanian architects, Rostrada.

BELOW A group of restoration consultants and art historians reviewing the metal plating samples

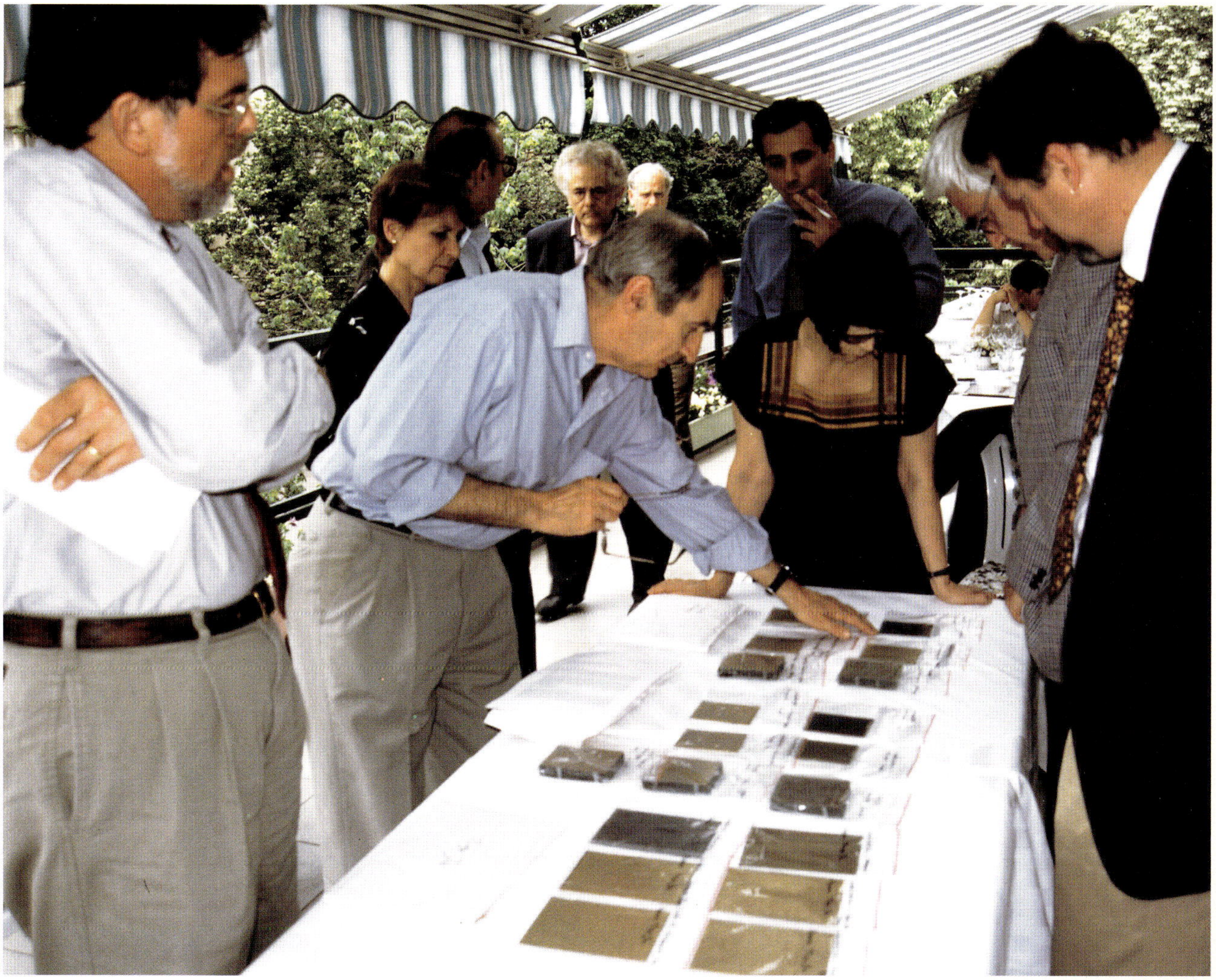

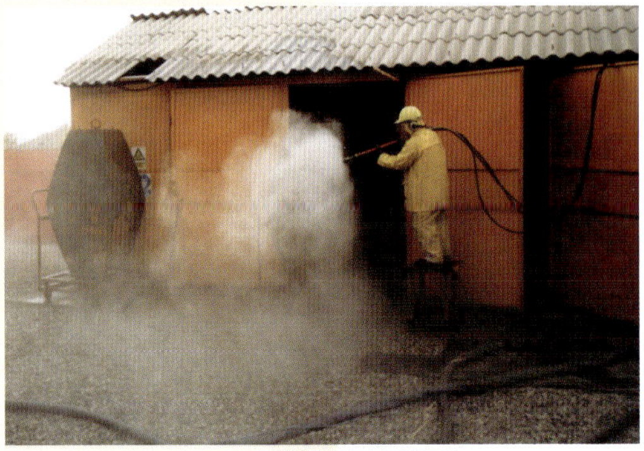
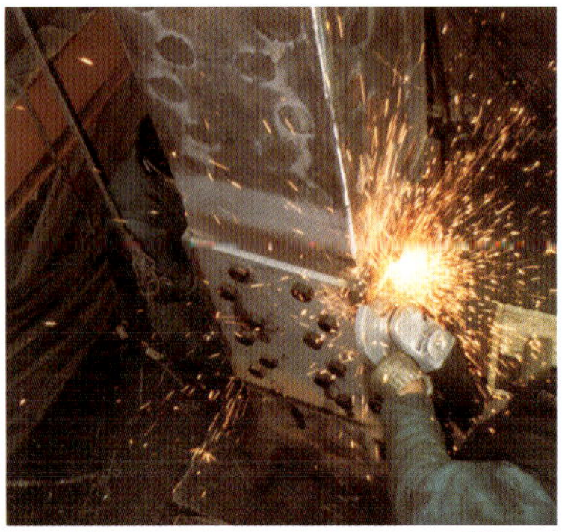
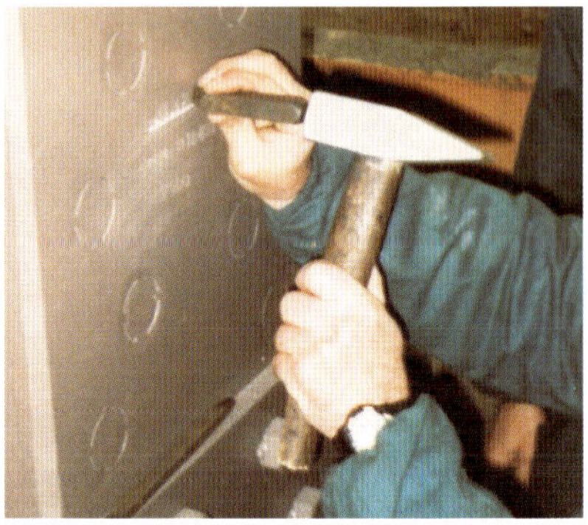
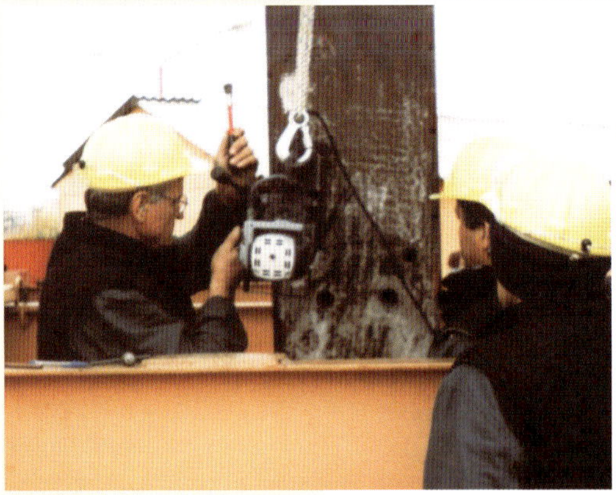
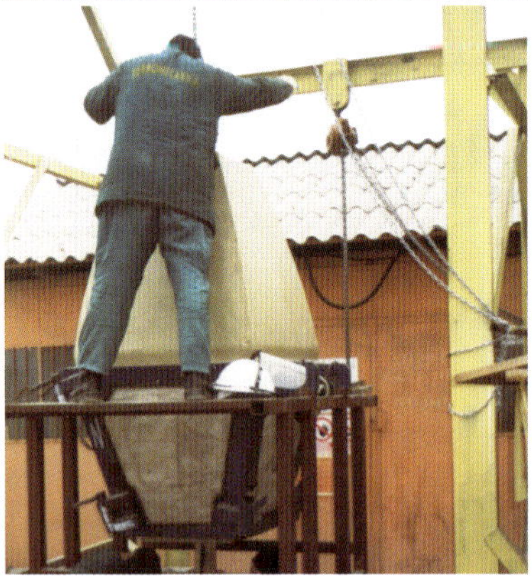
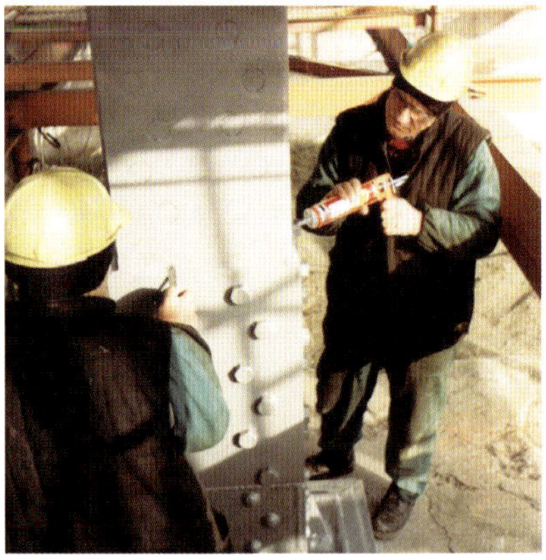

ABOVE Restorers at work, sand-blasting old metal-plating of the modules and welding new base plates at the base of the spine

RIGHT Protective wrapping during restoration of the *Column*

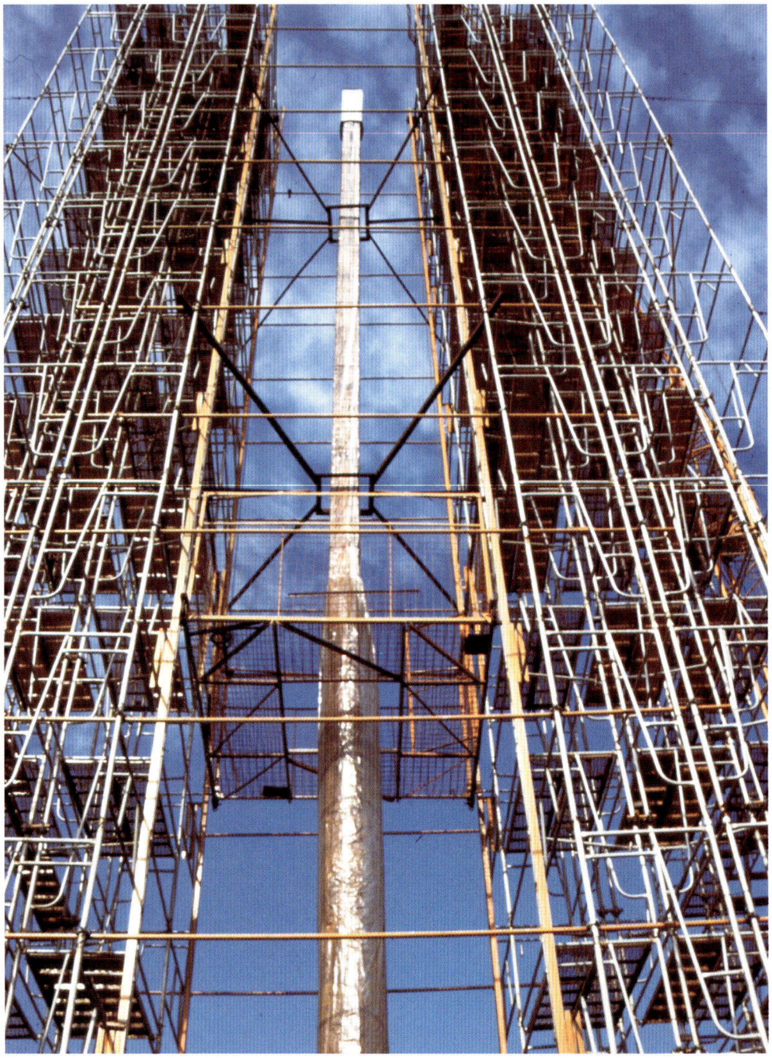

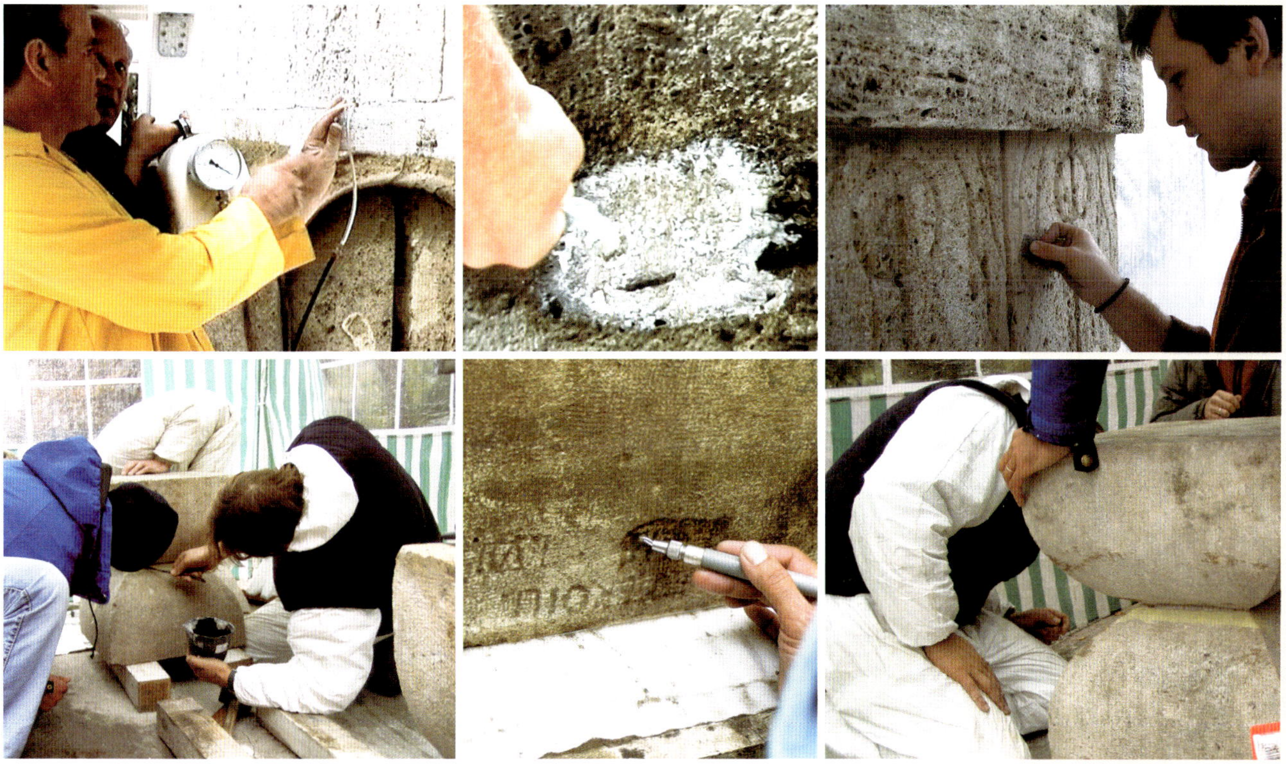

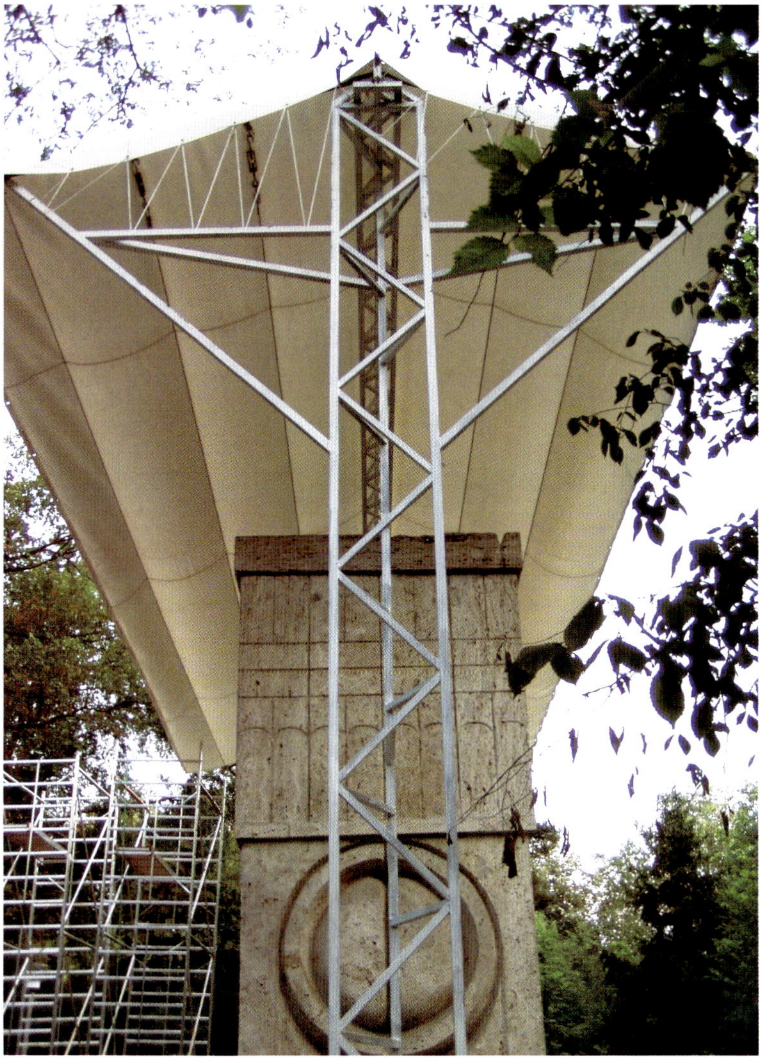

TOP The cleaning of the stone monuments, repair of the stools from the *Table of Silence* and removal of graffiti from the stone monuments

LEFT Protection scaffolding of the *Gate of the Kiss* during the restoration process

In 1998, the Romanian Government and WMF established a new partnership with the World Bank to finance the restoration of the ensemble, which would cost an estimated $3.6 million. The World Bank committed $2.6 million to the overall project in the form of a loan to the Romanian government; the WMF initially committed $600,000, but eventually raised more than $1 million from companies, foundations and private individuals. The Romanian Government and the town of Târgu Jiu provided additional funds as in-kind support.

A turning point in the project occurred at a technical meeting of 32 leading architects, engineers, art historians, government officials and conservators from five countries, which was held on 2–4 June 1999, in Târgu Jiu and Bucharest. Two of the most painstaking determinations would be the selection of the appropriate re-plating material and the decision as to whether to keep or replace the *Column*'s original steel spine. After long debates and numerous inspections of the *Column*'s existing condition, the meeting culminated in a final session in Bucharest, chaired by the Minister of Culture, Ion Caramitru. At this final meeting, it was agreed that while the cast-iron modules were in generally good structural condition, the original metal plating had failed completely in a number of areas and revealed a rusting substrate.

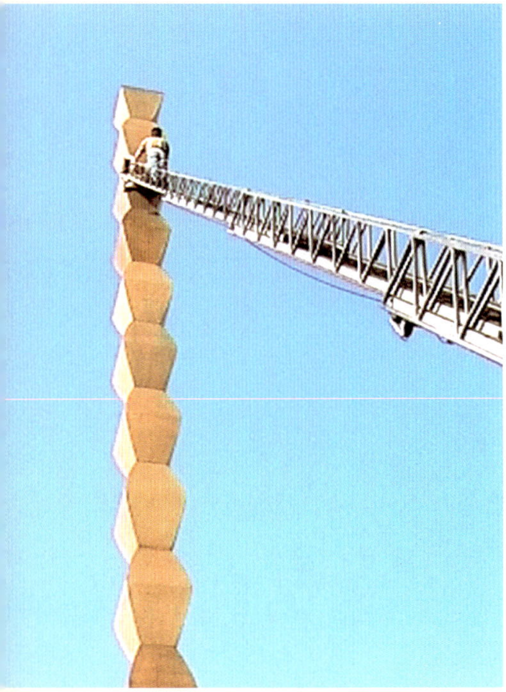

ABOVE The final inspection and touch-ups for the *Endless Column*

OPPOSITE Detail of the *Endless Column* following restoration

The 15 full and two half-modules of cast iron were originally plated in 1938 with a 'very pure golden-yellow' brass finish over a zinc base, as per Brancusi's instructions. After many alloys were tested, the final decision was to restore the modules with a metal plating identical to the original – a medium-yellow brass alloy sprayed on a base coat of zinc and polished by hand. In order to protect the modules from discoloration, a clear lacquer would be applied as a final protective coating.

The spine, a carbon-steel structure 28.3-metres high, cantilevers out of the ground; the modules are threaded onto it like a strand of pearls. The spine is made up of three sections, each approximately ten-metres high. The lowest section is a steel box section filled with concrete; the second one is a similar box section without the concrete fill; and the last section is a steel latticework. After close inspection of the spine, the structural engineers agreed to conserve (as opposed to replace) the original spine, which they determined was in relatively good condition, with the exception of four steel plates about two metres in height at the base of the spine, which would be replaced as a precautionary measure. In addition to cleaning the spine and replacing the suspect plates, they also recommended that an anti-corrosive layer be applied to the whole spine.

In the spring of 2000 two Romanian companies were selected through a competitive bidding process to carry out the work: U.A.P. (Uniunea Artistilor Plastici) would prepare the technical documents, while Turbomecanica would undertake the actual restoration of the *Endless Column*. With Turbomecanica completing the restoration work in less than four months, the restored *Endless Column* could be unveiled in December 2000. The *Column*'s reassembly and restoration brought it in line with modern safety codes and ensured its survival. In 2001 the *Endless Column* project was awarded the Europa Nostra Diploma for an outstanding restoration project.

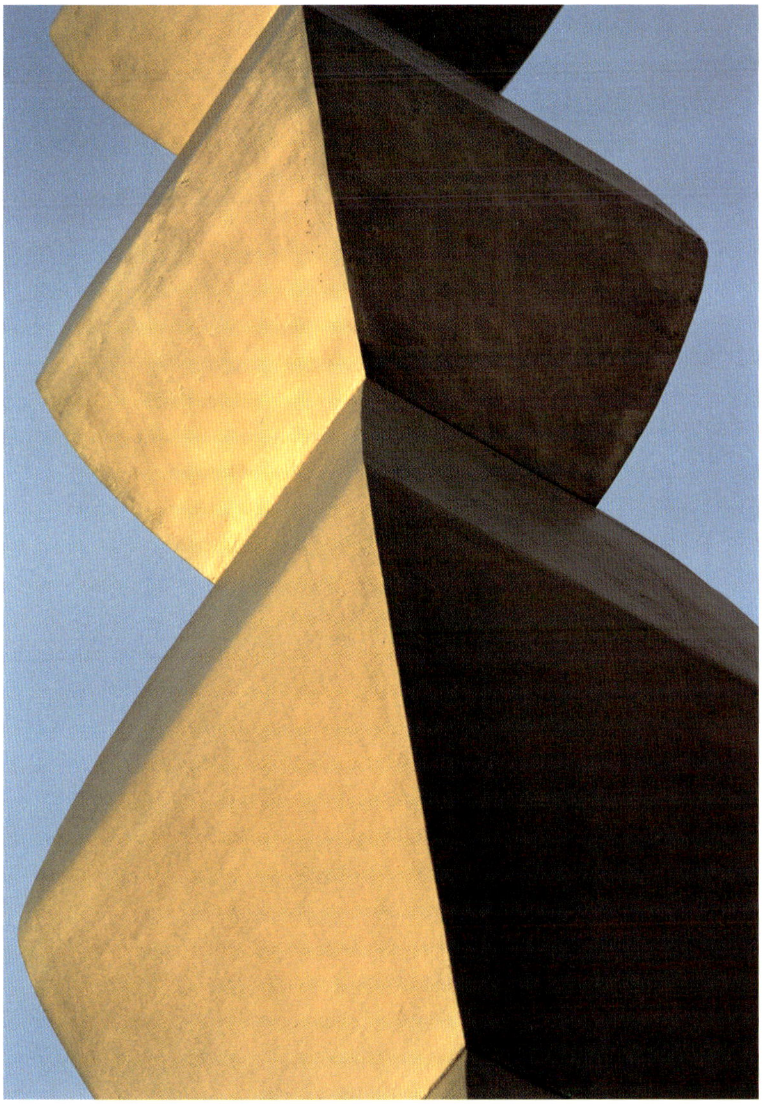

An event celebrating the completed restoration of the *Column* provided added impetus for restoring the two remaining components of the ensemble – the *Table of Silence* and *Gate of the Kiss* – and the Allée of Stools. For these subsequent projects, the monuments were surveyed, analysed and restored, in a collaboration between Italian conservator Paulo Pagnin and experts from the University of Architecture and Urban Design 'Ion Mincu', Bucharest.

By 2004, the travertine sculptures had been cleaned and restored. Travertine naturally displays numerous cavities; however, all the stone monuments were in good condition, with no evidence of scaling or other major alteration of the stone. Some of the joints between the stone blocks at the *Gate of the Kiss* were fractured, probably due to some small structural movements within the monument. The experts considered that the fractures in the stone were not endangering the structures, and they were left untouched. Some minor graffiti on the surface of the *Table of Silence* was removed, and the base of the seats and the table were cleaned and treated, as they had accumulated microbiological growth.

Reclaiming Sacred Space

Richard Newton

At a time when there is much debate about landscape as art, Constantin Brancusi's monumental ensemble holds particular significance for the landscape architect. Its location marks the place along the River Jiu where young Romanian soldiers made the ultimate sacrifice during World War I, and draws out from there a processional way, which continues through the town for over a mile. It is a sublime creation suggesting the journey from this life to the next, with a sequence of evocative, abstracted monuments placed within the fabric of everyday civic life. Commemorating a profoundly heroic and tragic moment in the history of Târgu Jiu and Romania as a nation, this seminal work of modern art is regarded as one of the first and most successful public monuments of the twentieth century.

Upon its completion, the ensemble defined a sacred space that stretched from the river floodplain to a hay market on the edge of town. The monuments punctuated a serene landscape of gently rolling hills, cultivated fields and farmhouses built of wood and stone, which were embraced by the snow-capped Carpathians in the distance. Since then, however, the ensemble has lost a substantial amount of its presence, yielding to visual clutter and landscape intrusions as the town continues to expand. The Avenue of the Heroes is now a major thoroughfare, bisected by other streets and lined with Soviet-era buildings, while the sculptures have been isolated from each other. The *Table of Silence* and *Gate of the Kiss* are located in the Municipal Park, which bustles with activity throughout the year. The Endless Column Park, which is much less used, abuts a school, a relatively tall and grim clothing factory, some houses and, further along the road to Bucharest, army barracks.

Following restoration of the sculptural elements in 2000, our team of landscape architects from the Philadelphia-based Olin Partnership, assisted by Bucharest-based associate architects, Rostrada, set out to restore the dignity and serenity that the work possessed prior to World War II. While it would be impossible to recreate the landscape of Brancusi's day, we could subtly alter the immediate surroundings of the ensemble in such a way that its power could be felt, despite a plethora of visual and aural distractions.

OPPOSITE *Table of Silence* set in a new surface of crushed stone, following landscape restoration, 2006

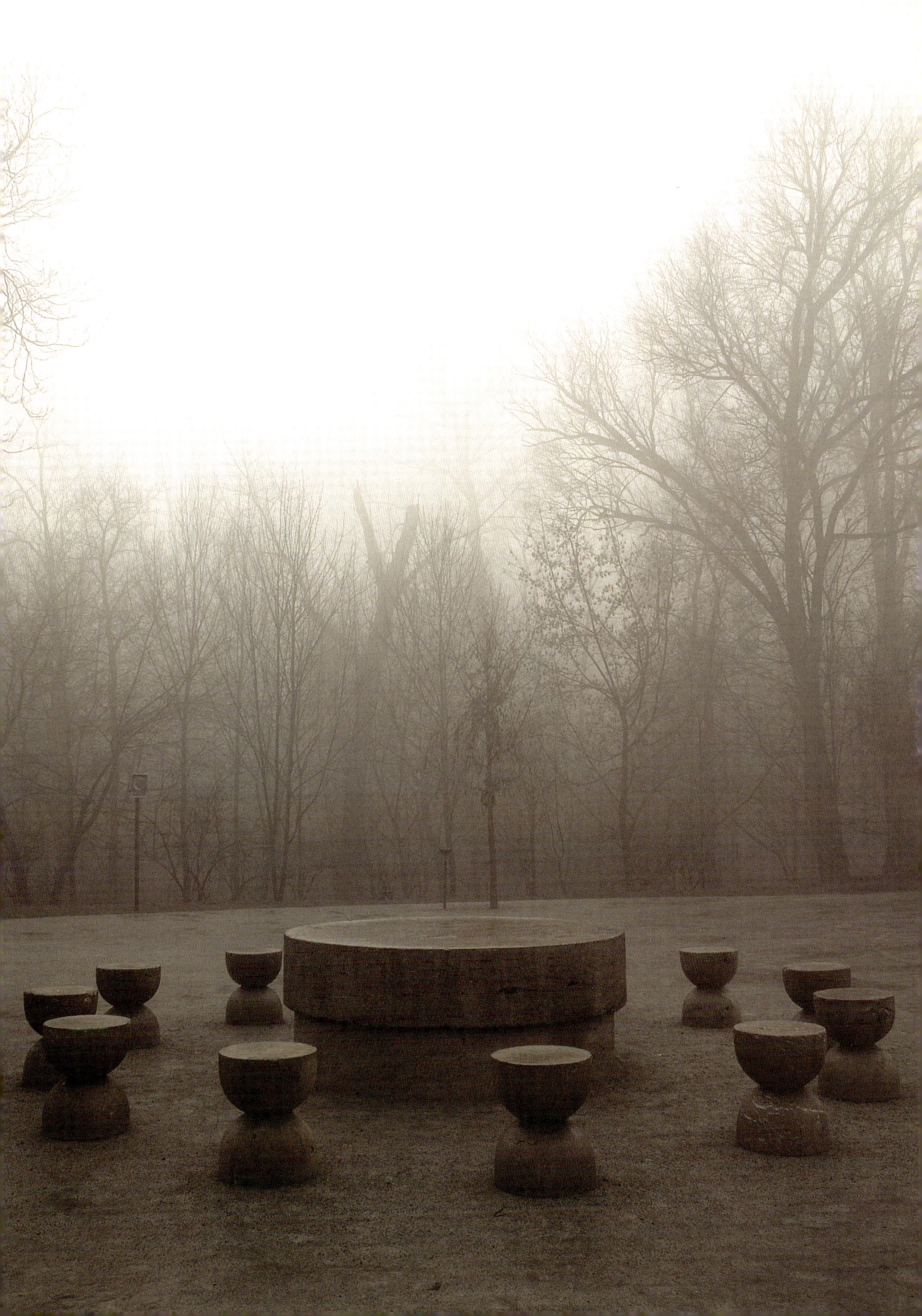

MUNICIPAL PARK: *TABLE OF SILENCE, GATE OF THE KISS* AND ALLÉE OF STOOLS

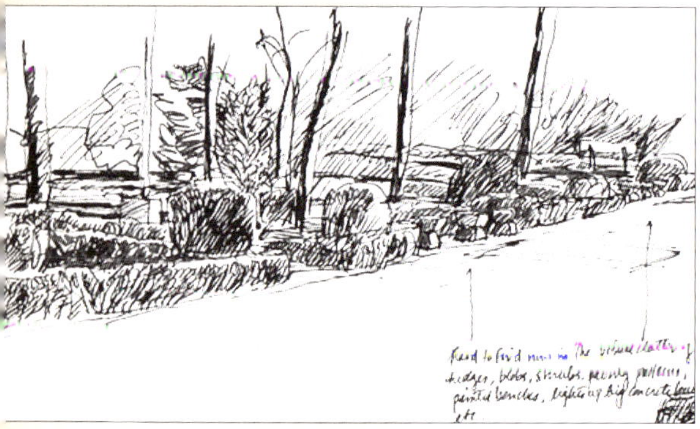

Sketch by Laurie Olin drawn on site to show how the background clutter undermined views of the stools, 2002

The *Table of Silence*, with its 12 vacant stools, originally stood on the banks of the River Jiu. However, since then the relationship between the sculpture and the river has been visually and physically obscured by a tall, grassy embankment installed as part of a flood control measure when the river was dammed. The embankment itself was planted with black poplars, while a visually distracting water feature located at its base competed for attention. Moreover, low hedges had been planted around the sculpture, further diminishing its presence.

Our goal was to create a calm, reflective and sacred space in which the *Table* could sit quietly apart from the park, making it a destination rather than a thoroughfare. To do this, we removed all of the hedges, opting instead for a single, soft-edged ellipse of crushed stone around the table and stools, beyond which we planted a grove of weeping willows that, with their long hanging branches that move with the gentlest breeze, are associated with mourning and water. In time, the willows will grow together to form a loosely defined and separate space from the surrounding park.

The Allée of Stools (a 160-metre-long path lined with 15 stools on each side), connecting the *Table of Silence* with the *Gate of the Kiss*, is lined with horse chestnuts. Although these dramatically framed the space, the trees had grown in a way that shaded the stools, placing them in shadow for much of

Table of Silence following stone restoration, but prior to the landscape work in 2002. The surrounding hedges, the telegraph poles and water feature behind provide unwelcome clutter to what should be a contemplative setting

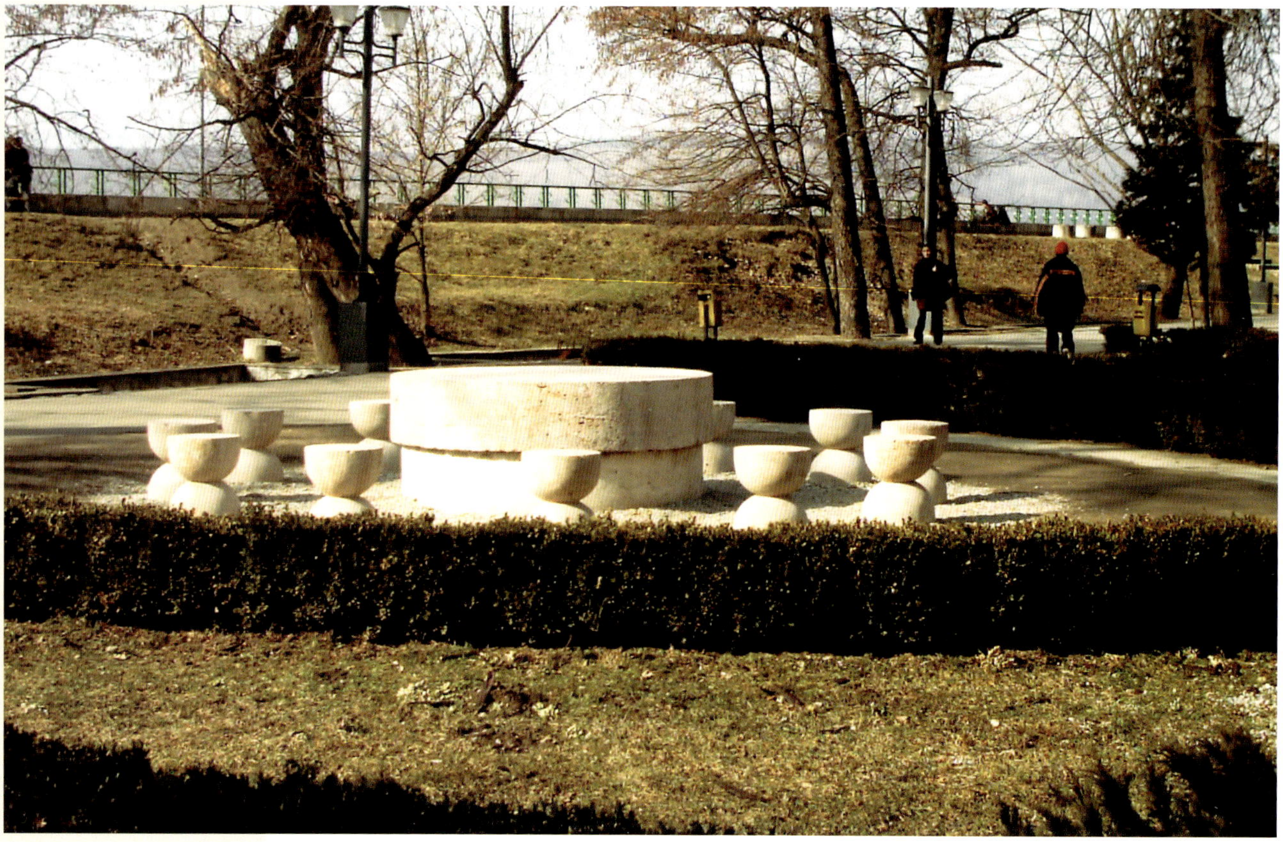

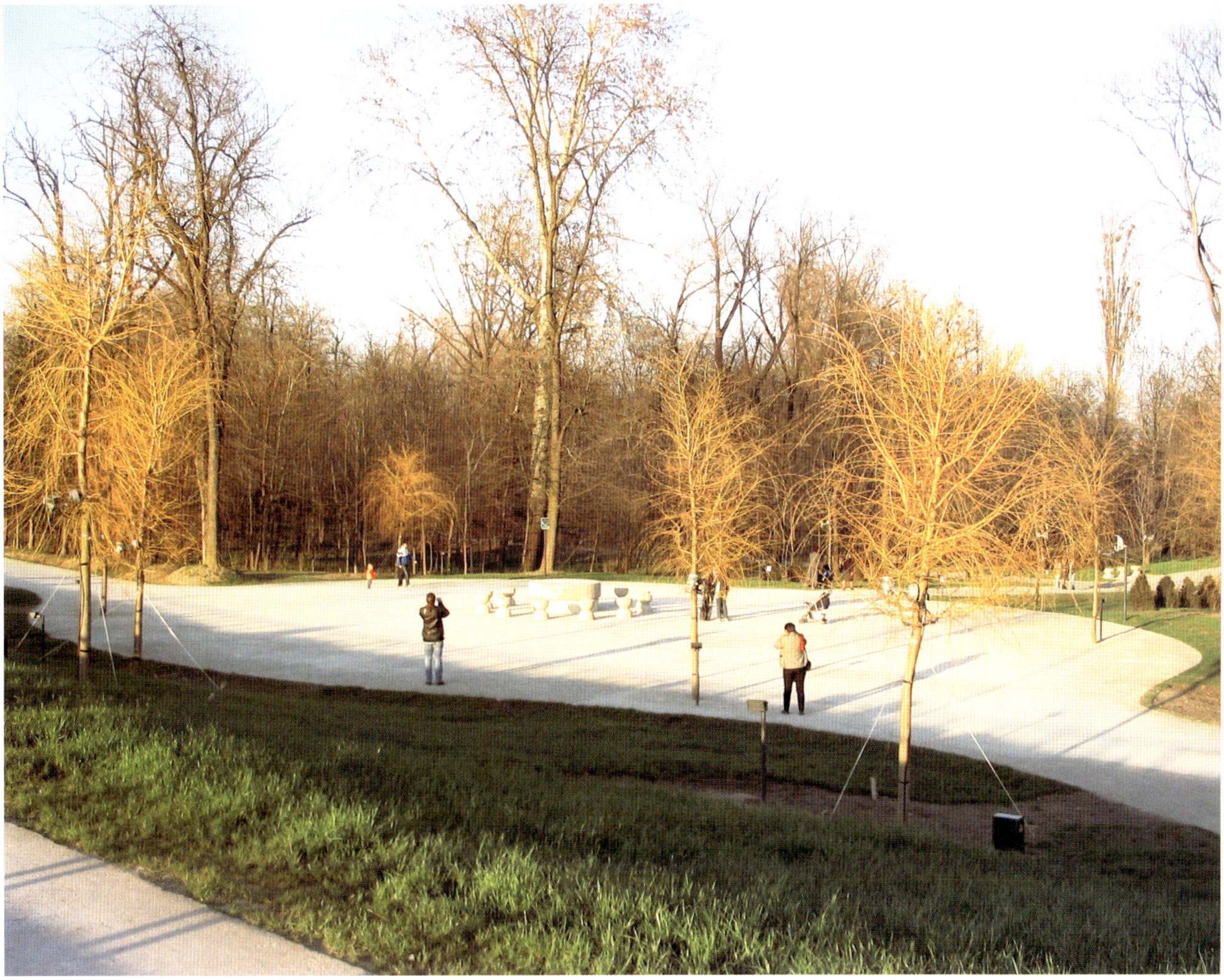

In its new landscape setting, the *Table* is seen in late-afternoon light during winter. Over time the grove of weeping willows will grow to frame the space around the table

the day. Moreover, small low-clipped hedges had been planted around the stools, making them all but invisible in the surrounding visual clutter. The allée was also crossed by three paths: two were important park circulation routes, but one – which crossed the path between the gate and the stools – was particularly intrusive and of lesser importance for pedestrian movement, and was therefore omitted. Beyond the allée, on either side, were dark areas of woodland and, close to the gate, a children's playground. The allée, originally of bare earth, had been paved in the Ceaucescu era with crude concrete displaying a decorative pattern, and it was in very poor condition.

To allow the stools to be clearly seen and to return the ensemble to its more rural character, the hedges were removed and background distractions were carefully screened by planting soft bands of shade-tolerant shrubs behind the stools, in three rows of increasing height. The species were chosen to provide subtly varying seasonal colours and textures. For the walking surface, the same crushed stone that was used around the *Table* was extended along the allée and edged with a matching coloured kerb. Carefully proportioned recesses of crushed stone frame each group of three stools, while the remaining areas have been planted with grass.

RIGHT Before the restoration, the setting of the *Gate* was very well used by residents, but was in poor condition with uneven and cracked concrete paving

BELOW RIGHT The crushed stone paving uses stone from the same source as the sculptures and provides a sympathetic surface, which in summer reflects light up into the tree canopy

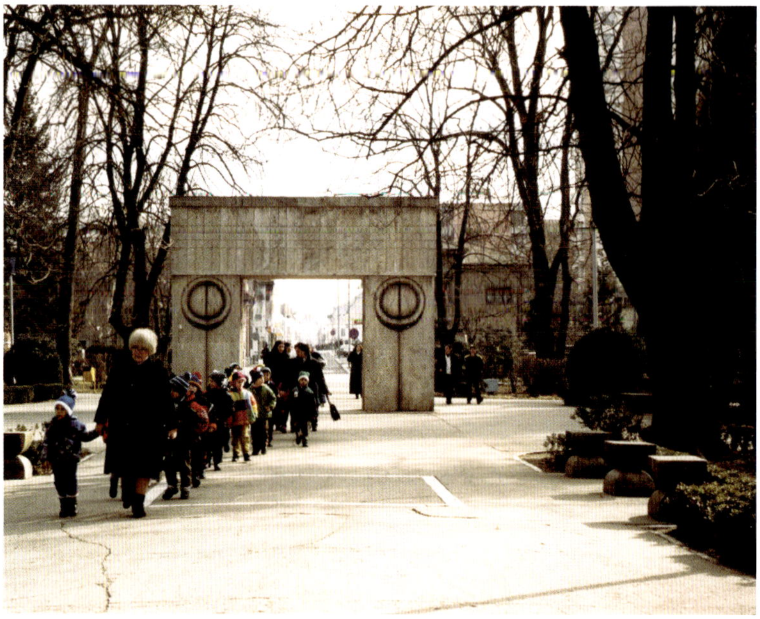

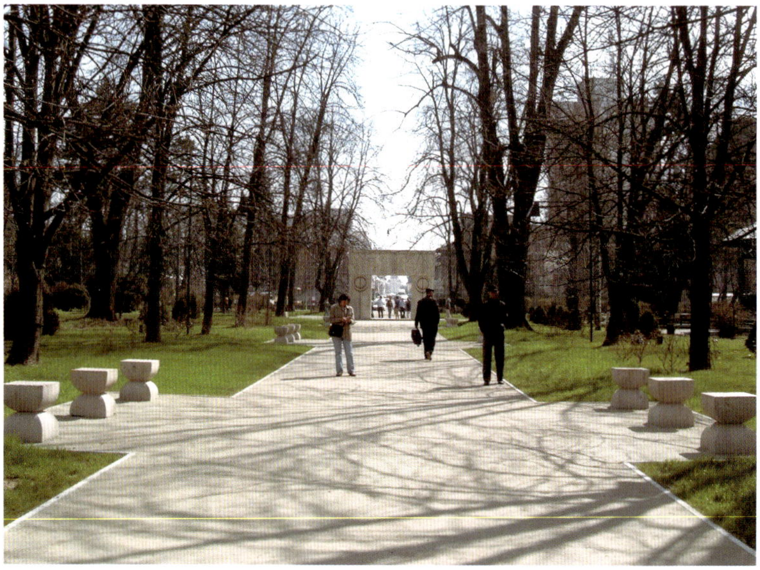

Much thought and debate went into the choice of material for the paths. Aside from practical considerations of maintenance, the discussion focused on finding a material that was robust and yet rustic in feel, and easy to maintain. We wanted to respond to the primal quality of the work by choosing a material that would reflect light up to the underside of the tree canopy, yet one that did not have an insistent pattern. After viewing many samples of crushed stone, we opted for the same stone from which the stools were made for all paths within the two parks associated with the ensemble.

Finally the horse chestnuts were carefully pruned to filter more light down to the stools. Continued annual pruning will ensure that there is sufficient light during the day. For night-time illumination, lights were placed high within the foliage of the trees and were suspended from discreet poles placed apart from the stools between the tree trunks.

OPPOSITE The *Gate of the Kiss* frames the view to the Orthodox church in the distance, along the Avenue of the Heroes, 2006

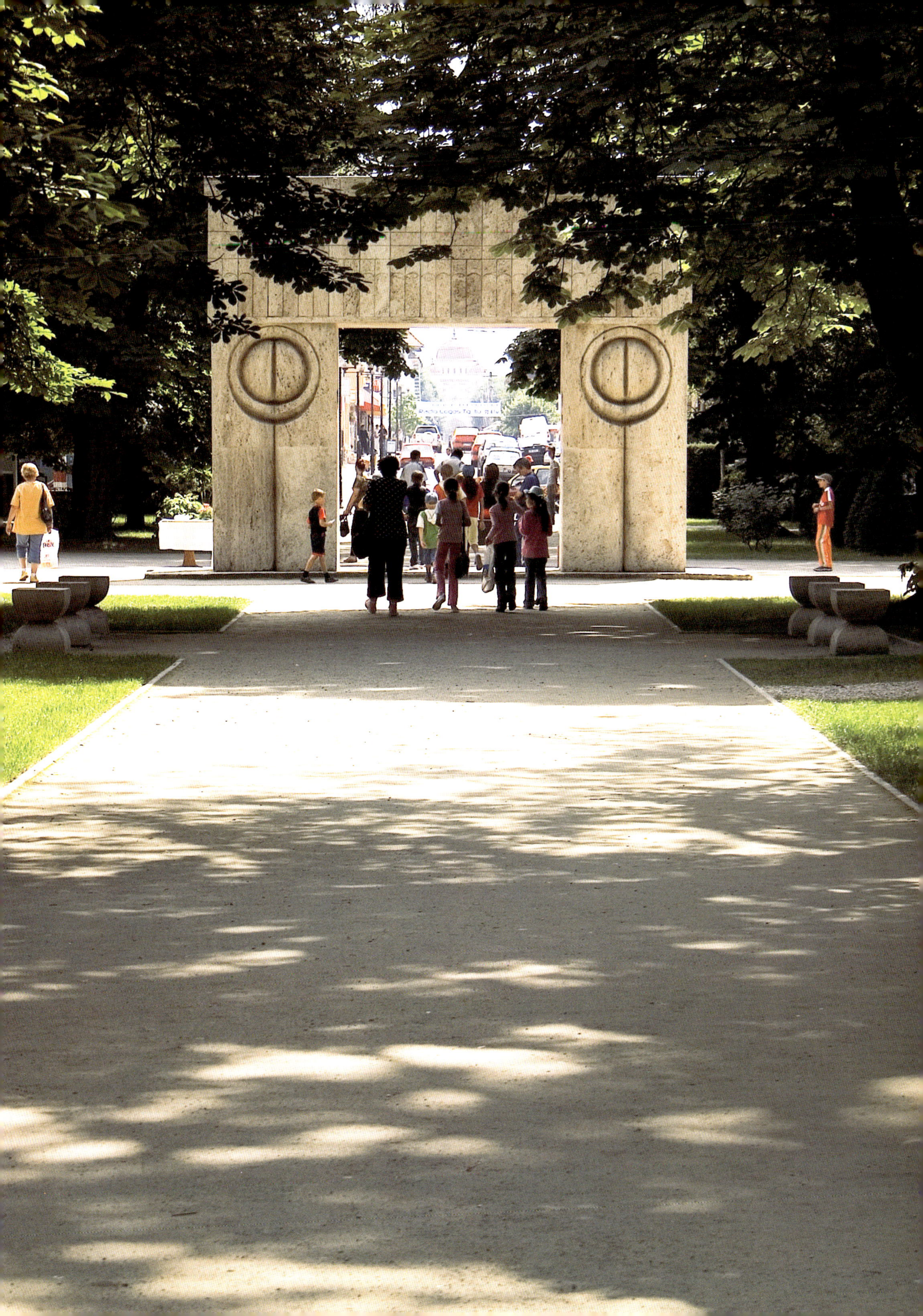

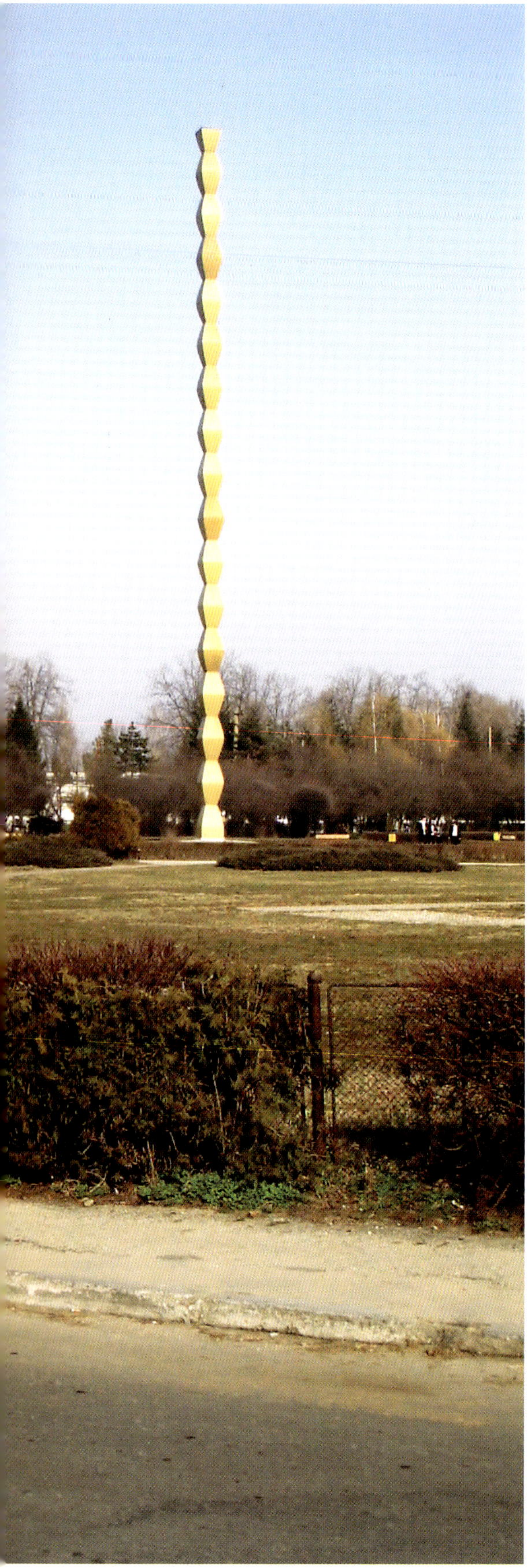
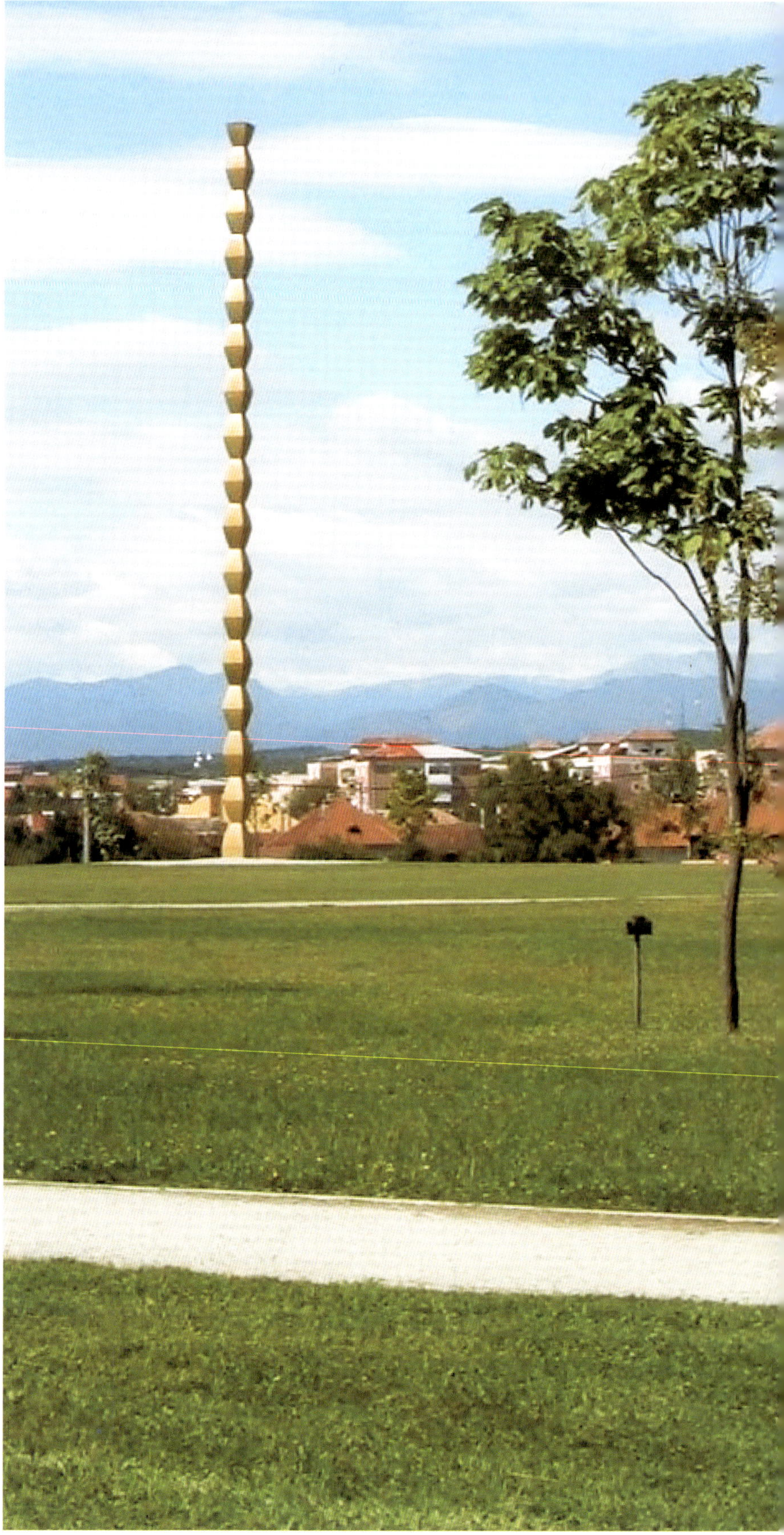

Originally the site of a hay market outside the town, today the Endless Column Park is a long triangular space with roads on each side. Although the *Column* dominated the space around, the park was poorly defined and not in good condition. In addition, as time passed, most views of the sculpture invariably showed buildings in the background that detracted from the idea of the *Column's* connection with the infinite.

The *Column*, and in particular its connection to the sky, is the culmination of the procession from the river. To reinforce this connection, a variety of large and small trees have been planted at a distance of approximately one-and-a-half times the *Column*'s height to form a seasonally changing backdrop and to screen out the surrounding buildings. Over time, these small trees will grow together to form a woodland around the *Column*, which is open to the north-west, to provide a view of the distant Carpathian Mountains. When the trees mature, they will frame the sculpture in such a way that, approached from the Avenue of the Heroes, it will once again be seen against the vast horizon, distant mountains and sky.

The whole topography of the park has been subtly altered so that the *Column* appears to rise from a high point. This high point at the base of the *Column* is a simple circle of the same crushed stone used in the Municipal Park and the paths that encirle the *Column*. The paths are located on the periphery of the clearing around the *Column*, so that visitors see it at a distance and without any adjacent element against which to judge its scale. The paths are lowered and set in the shade of the woodland edge so that they are recessive and do not interupt the visual continuity of the ground surface. The approach to the *Column* is via grass paths mown each season through the

OPPOSITE In these before and after photographs of the *Column*, although taken from different viewpoints, the new landscape simplifies the foreground and allows a more legible connection between the *Column* and ground. This view will improve over time as the surrounding trees mature and the urban context is screened

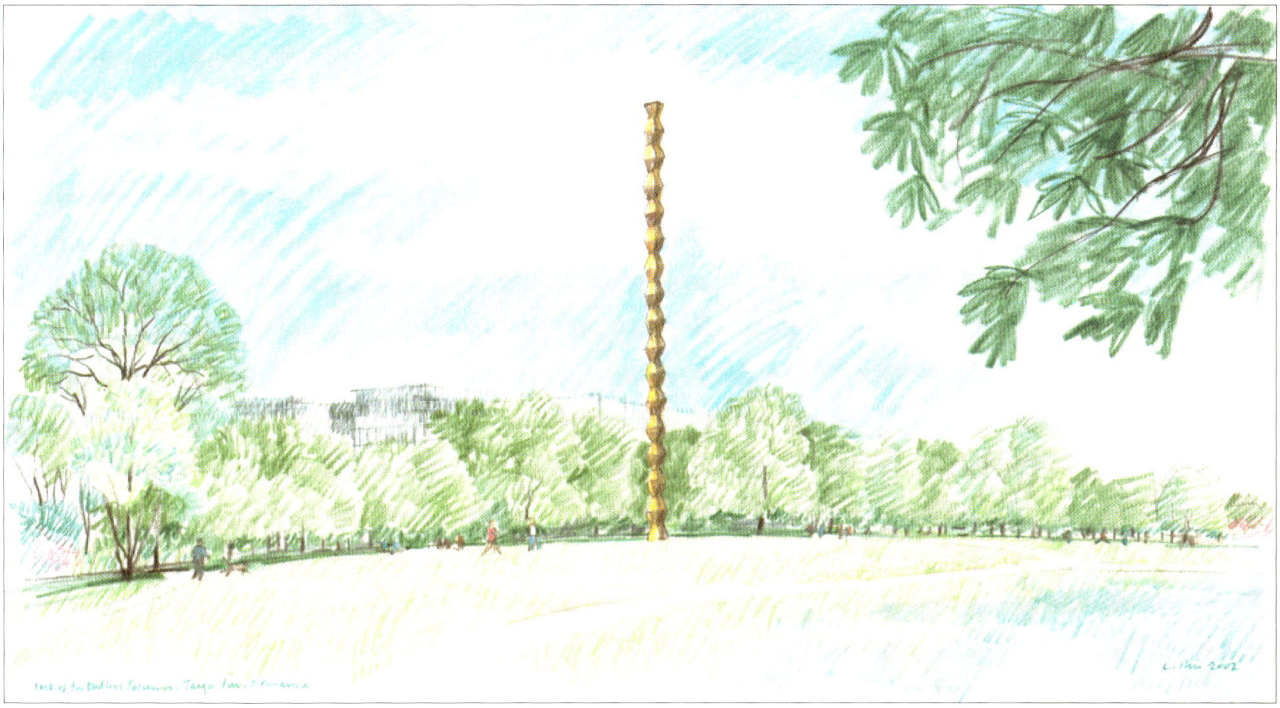

BELOW Sketch of the maturing landscape, 2002, showing the *Endless Column* against a woodland backdrop and set on gently rising ground, planted as a wildflower meadow. The mown curving paths will allow visitors to approach the *Column*

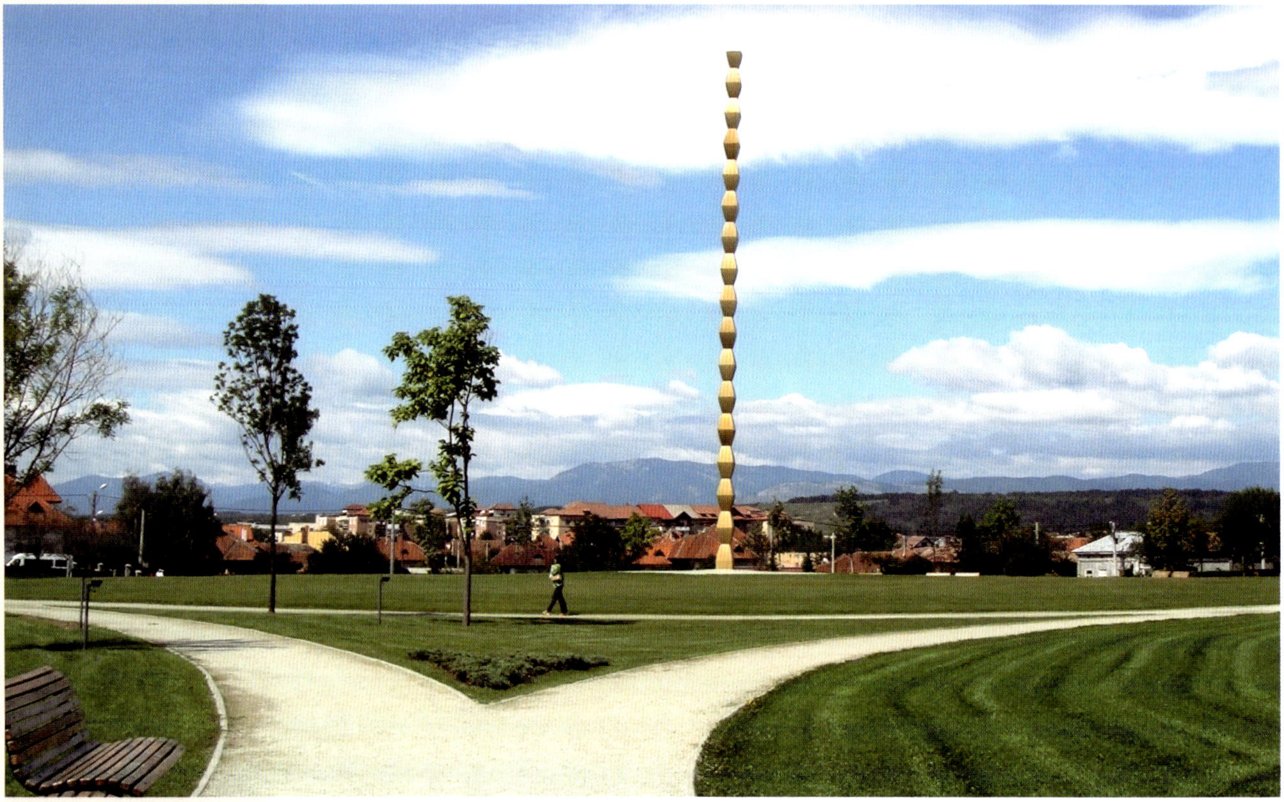

In this view from the east the *Column* is seen against a backdrop of the Carpathian Mountains. When mature, newly planted trees will frame the space and screen views of the surrounding buildings

surrounding meadow planted with native wildflowers, which in full bloom should reach about half a metre in height. Benches are located along the paths around the perimeter of the clearing and park. Beyond the *Column* to the east, where the park narrows, is a lawn of mown grass for playing and picnicking. The intent is to make this an informal recreational space for visitors and residents alike, one that relieves the pressure from the area around the *Column* for recreation and other park activities, and which also affords long views towards the sculpture. Within the trees are planned public facilities, including bathrooms, a café, a children's playground and a security and maintenance office.

AVENUE OF THE HEROES

With the exception of a handsome Orthodox church, which is located in the centre of the thoroughfare approximately halfway between the two parks, the Avenue of the Heroes is a road that has little to distinguish it from other roads in the town. Between the Municipal Park and the church, the street is dominated by modern concrete buildings erected during the later years of Ceaucescu's regime. These intrude on the more human scale of the older buildings and on the overall character of the street itself. The avenue is further interrupted by a large open swathe of municipal gardens, with roads on either side approximately one third of the way between the park and the church. This strong axial open space and its bombastic buildings distracts

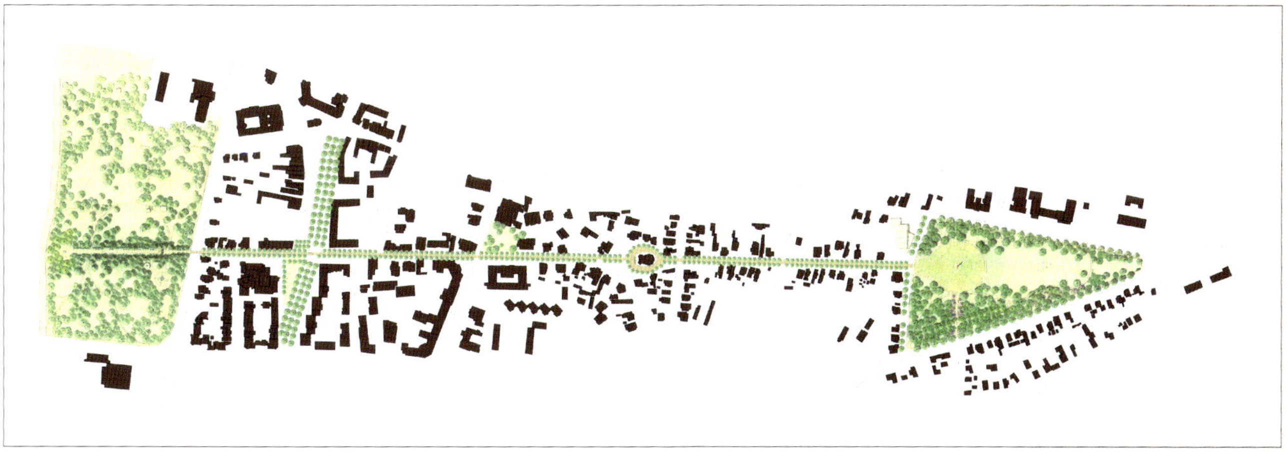

from the ensemble's processional axis. The *Endless Column* becomes visible just after passing the church, at which point the street takes on a more rural and coherent character reminiscent of Brancusi's day, with one- and two-storey houses with gardens amid traditional fences. This calm approach to the climax of the sequence created by Brancusi is rudely interrupted, however, by railway tracks and occasional commuter and freight trains. Throughout the length of the street, particularly between the Municipal Park and the church, road traffic detracts from the experience.

Landscape master plan, 2002, showing a stronger connection between the Municipal Park (left) and the Endless Column Park (right). Widened pavements and a line of street trees provide an attractive experience for pedestrians

We believe that the street should have a distinctive character, with locally available basalt blocks currently installed around the church and extended throughout the length of the street. To provide a more generous and attractive space for pedestrians, we have proposed that the pavements be widened and that vehicular access be managed so that only vehicles that need to access the street are allowed. We also suggested planting trees on either side of the avenue to give it a more sympathetic and humane character. This will also provide a consistently attractive edge and reinforce the ensemble's primary axis by providing a 'green' link between the two parks.

Beyond this, Mihai Radu of Radu Architects has completed an urban study for the immediate surrounding area that proposes new buildings and uses that are consistent with the character of the Avenue of the Heroes (see next chapter). In particular, at the end of the Avenue of the Heroes on the north side, a site has been chosen for a visitor centre, which will inform the visitor about Brancusi, his work and, in particular, the monumental ensemble and the history of Târgu Jiu.

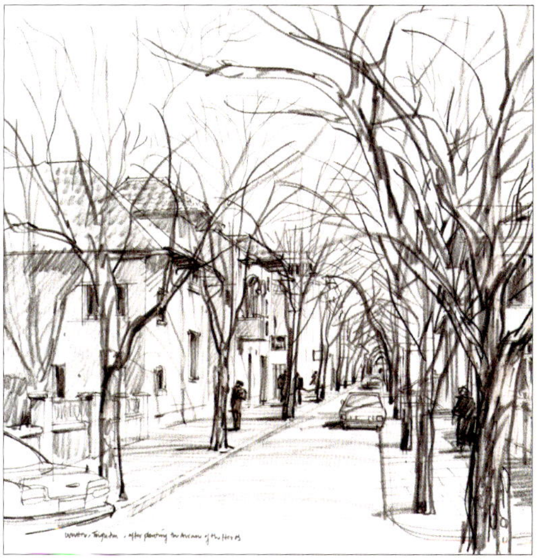

In this sketch of the Avenue of the Heroes (2002) seen from the Municipal Park, street tree-planting frames and strengthens the axis that leads to the Endless Column Park

While we cannot turn back the clock to an earlier era, the landscape design for this ensemble of abstract sculptures by Brancusi, which was originally placed in a rural setting, allows visitors to view them quietly and without the intrusion of the modern context. The design of the landscape has been an exercise in editing this context and clarifying the situation in order to allow Brancusi's work to dominate and once again be experienced as the coherent, powerful and spiritual ensemble the artist envisioned.

Urban Redevelopment and a Visionary New Visitor Centre

Mihai Radu

OPPOSITE The new lighting scheme lights the *Column* with a single powerful lamp from the base so that the top of the *Column* appears to gradually merge with the night sky

BELOW Brincoveanu-style building renovated by WMF as an orientation centre located in the Municipal Park

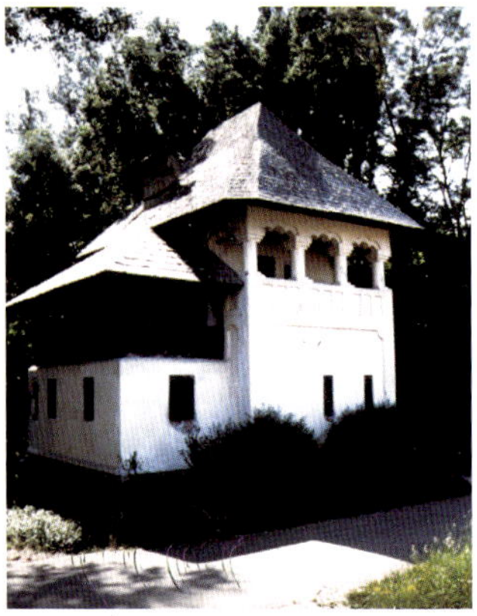

Brancusi was ahead of his time when he conceived the notion of transforming the urban landscape through the introduction of significant art elements – a technique later reflected in the monumental urban art of Isamu Noguchi, Mark Di Suvero, Alexander Calder, Richard Serra and others. Pioneered by Brancusi in the late 1930s, this concept of modern monumental public art as urban catalyst is still a valid urban theory today and has guided our work in planning for urban redevelopment.

Like many cities and towns in Romania, Târgu Jiu was dramatically affected by the socialist urban planning schemes of the Ceaucescu regime. Known as 'systematization', the goal was to reduce the entire citizenry to the same proletarian living standard, housed in large nondescript building units not unlike those that came to blight so many western cities in the 1960s. In Romania, systemization was achieved by razing the city centre, radically reconstructing it with stark avenues lined with huge, poorly constructed buildings, which have since declined into tenements. In Târgu Jiu itself, the main market street was demolished and re-oriented, with large-scale apartment blocks and an unsightly hotel tower, which occupies an area once filled with traditional vernacular buildings. This radical redesign has placed traffic pressure on the Avenue of the Heroes, which once ran perpendicular to the main street, but which now functions as the main thoroughfare. Today, in the town centre near the *Gate of the Kiss*, the visitor confronts a mix of poorly maintained paving, dishevelled mass housing, jumbled signage and buildings of every size and description. As time passes and these buildings reach obsolescence, we believe that a new opportunity will emerge to re-establish the avenue as a place of peace and contemplation. The goal of our urban plan, therefore, is to take advantage of these opportunities and gain the participation of municipal authorities in implementing a new vision for the city.

While the landscaping of the Endless Column Park and the Municipal Park has done much to unify the core area around the monuments in an otherwise architecturally chaotic city, it is merely the start – the nucleus of an overall redevelopment scheme for the town, which will include the building

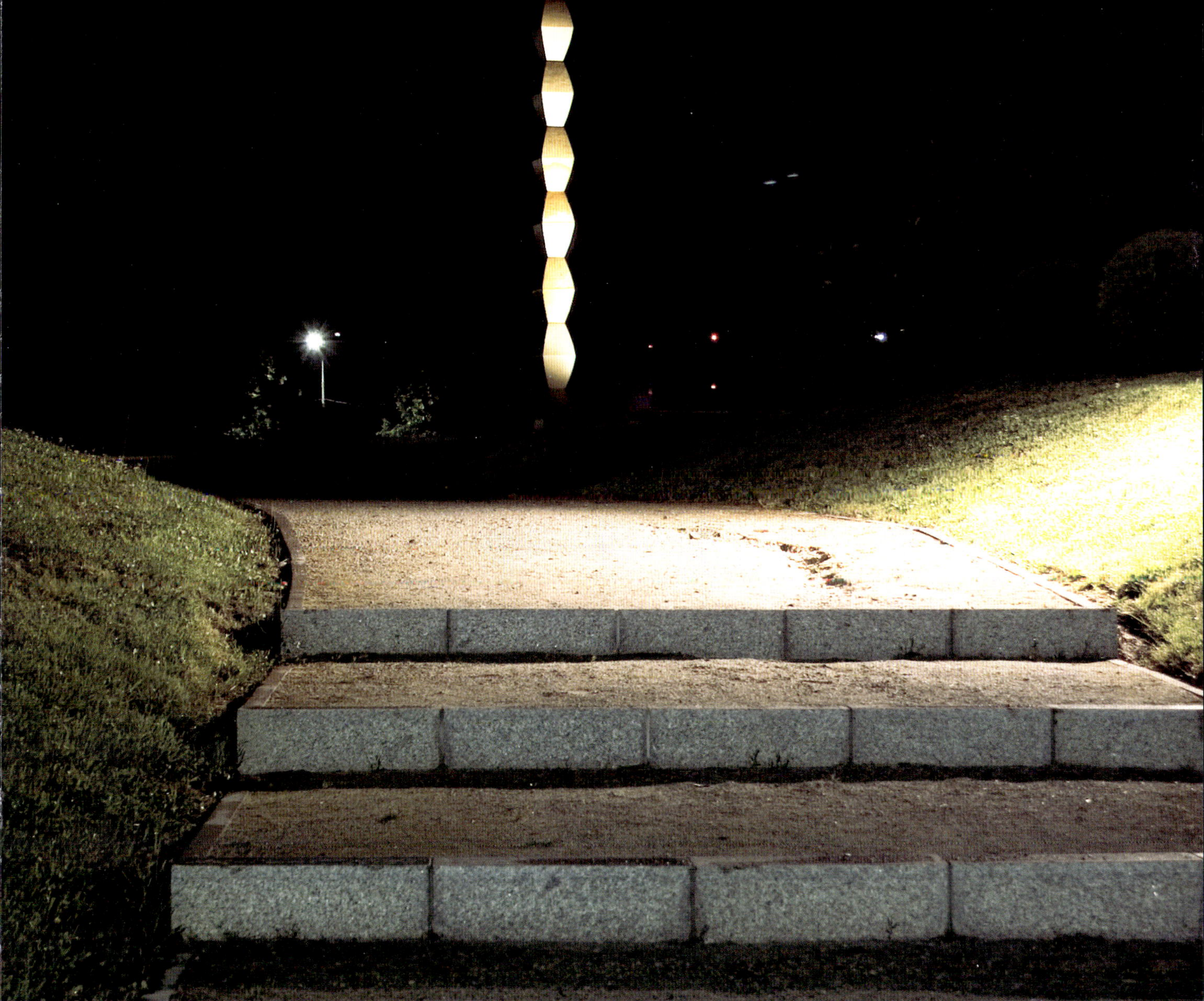

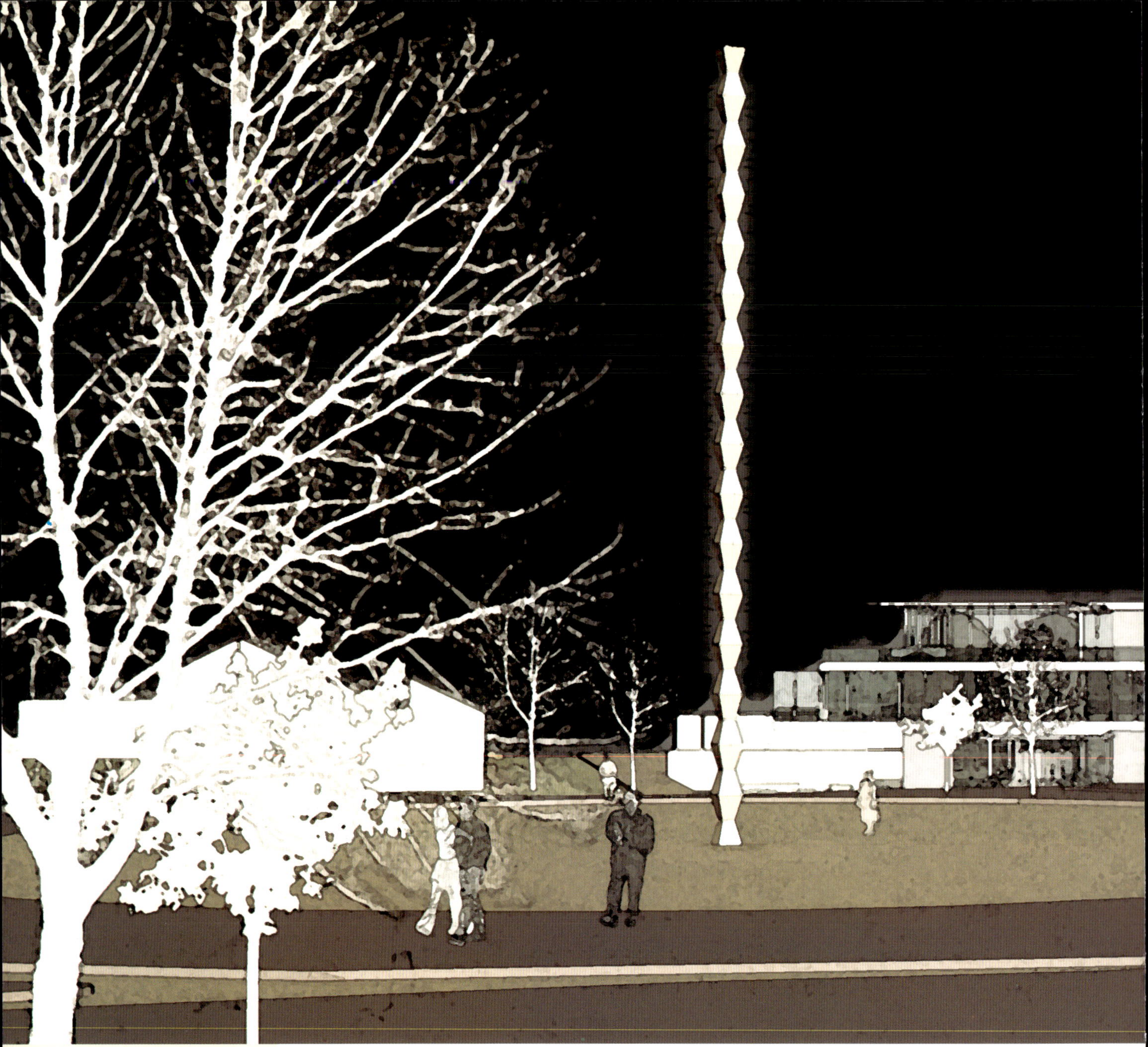

A rendering of one of several concepts proposed by Radu Architects (in 2007) for the new visitor centre near the Endless Column Park

of a new visitor centre near the *Endless Column* and, ultimately, an integration of the surrounding landscape.

In the interim, as part of the restoration of the monumental ensemble, WMF restored and updated an existing traditional house to create a small orientation centre at the south-western end of the Municipal Park, near the *Table of Silence* and *Gate of the Kiss*. The building's formal typology is of the Gorj region's traditional Brincoveanu-style *cula's*. These *cula's* are fortified houses with a high ground floor and observation terraces all around for defence and easy surveillance of the surroundings. The location is on the banks of the River Jiu, close to the administrative and business centre of the town. It therefore provides the first urban design link to draw attention to the role of the ensemble in the future shape of the town, and is consistent with Brancusi's original intent.

During the restoration project, we realized that a vacant lot, occupying a

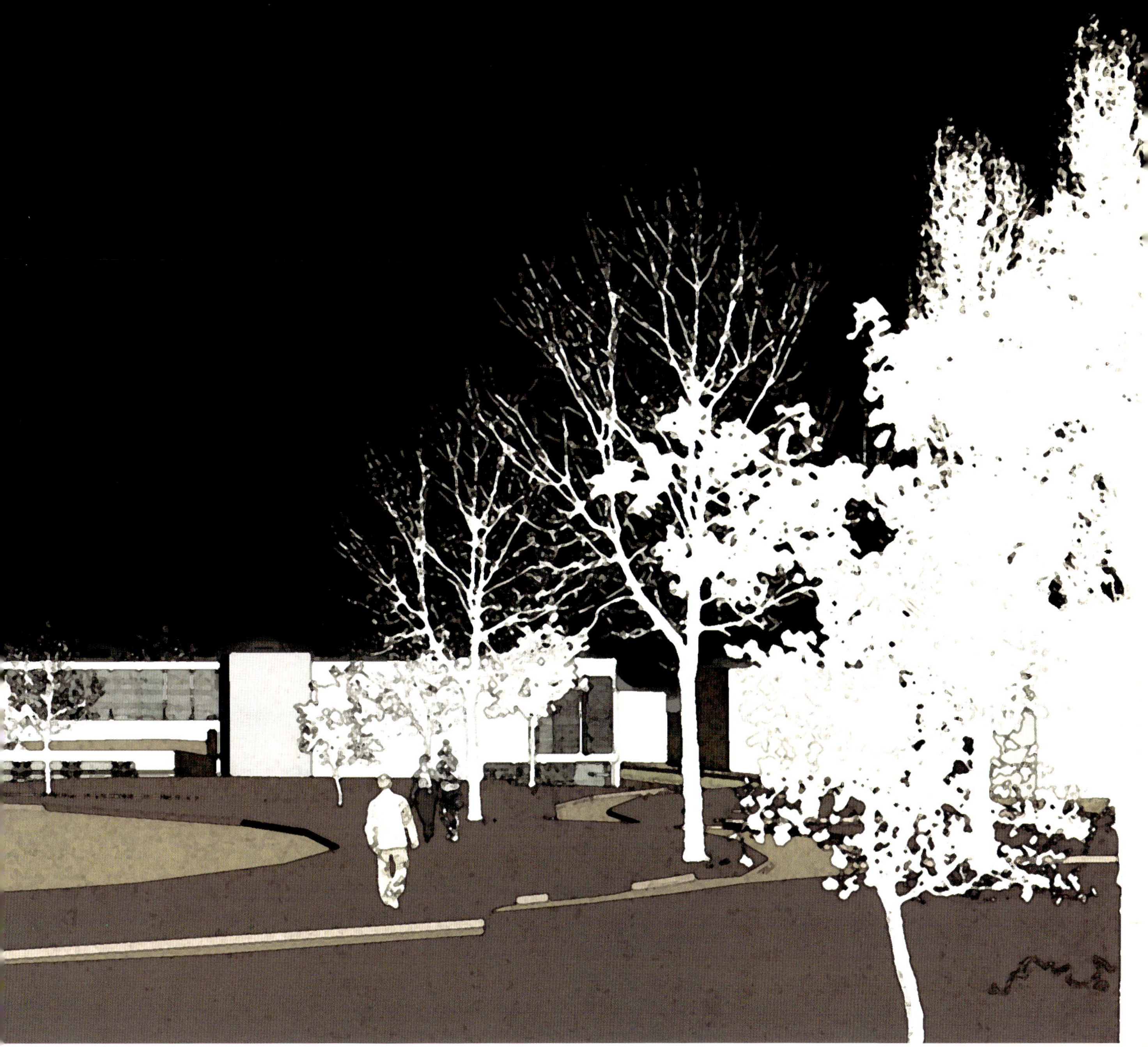

key position near the *Endless Column*, towards the town and the Carpathian Mountains beyond, would be an ideal location for our proposed visitor centre. To secure the site and avoid the possibility of the construction of another incompatible building near the ensemble, WMF patron Mica Ertegün formed the Infinitului Foundation in 2004. Beyond acquiring the site, the foundation will raise funds to finance the construction of the new centre. Beyond accommodating local and international visitors to the site, it will serve as a catalyst that will realign the focus of Târgu Jiu's future development in light of Brancusi's axis, and will complement the town's existing administrative and business centre. The incorporation of the eastern end of the Avenue of the Heroes into the town's cultural and business life will also boost the entire area defined by the two parks.

During construction of the centre, set for completion by 2010, additional urban infastructure improvements will resolve the Communist-era

RIGHT Târgu Jiu town centre

OPPOSITE Proposed urban planning scheme for future development of the centre of Târgu Jiu, showing the three stages of development. Phase A is a diagram of the first 5 years; Phase B represents the next 5–15 years' development; and Phase C, 15–30 years

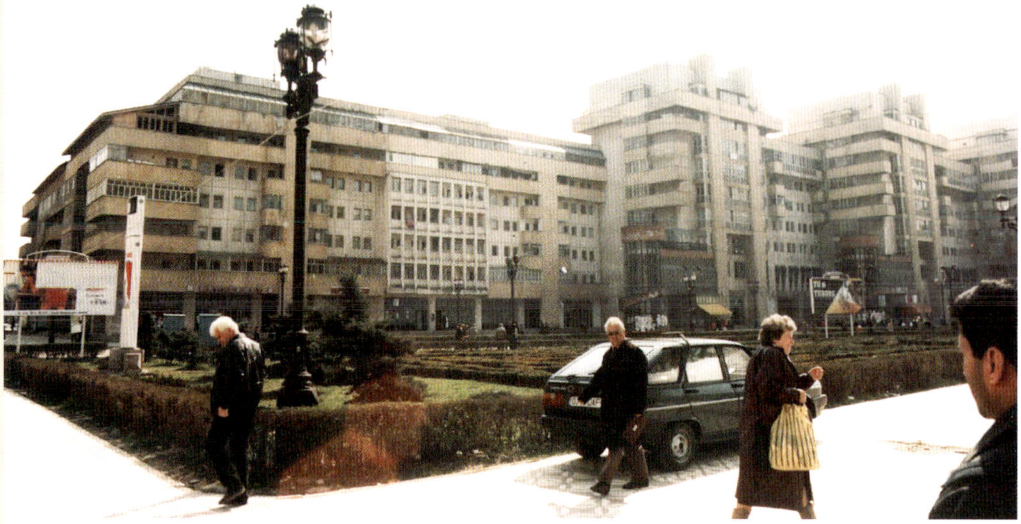

urban confusion by clarifying and redefining the pedestrian and vehicular experience of the ensemble, and reincorporating Brancusi's work into the life of the city. This will be achieved by the redesign of the Avenue of the Heroes, which encourages visitors to walk between the two parks and enjoy the town's historic district, together with the reconfiguration of the town centre that is more respectful of the original urban fabric.

The goal of the new centre itself is to enhance a visitor's understanding of Brancusi's genius in the context of Târgu Jiu. Its design language will pay homage to Brancusi's use of Romanian vernacular ornament by incorporating some of the artist's trademark elements – clear, powerful volumes interlocked through carefully selected proportions; materials that are faithful to Brancusi's use of stone and metal. The centre will also provide visitors with an opportunity to learn about the construction of the ensemble, and to contemplate the *Endless Column* from a new perspective. It will also serve as an ideal venue for exhibitions by contemporary artists inspired by Brancusi's example as one of the most innovative artists of the twentieth century.

In the end, our hope is that beyond the restoration and renovation project itself, new architectural and landscaping elements in the city – part of an urban design master plan – will further enhance the great sense of pride the ensemble's restoration has returned to the local community, and the new hope it portends for Târgu Jiu.

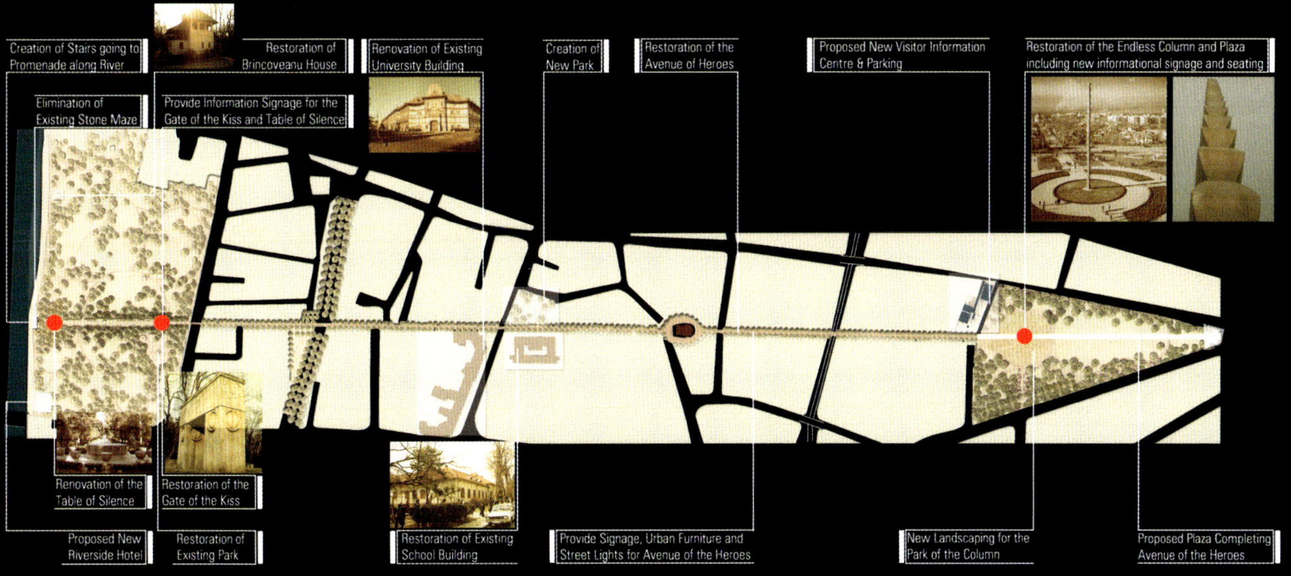

Phase B

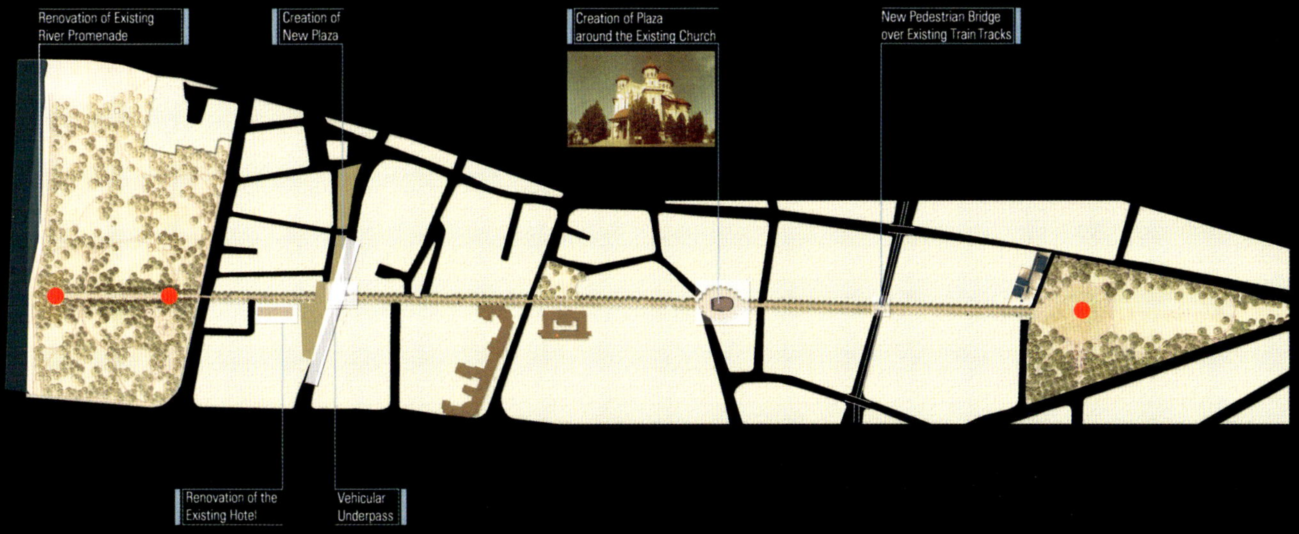

Phase C

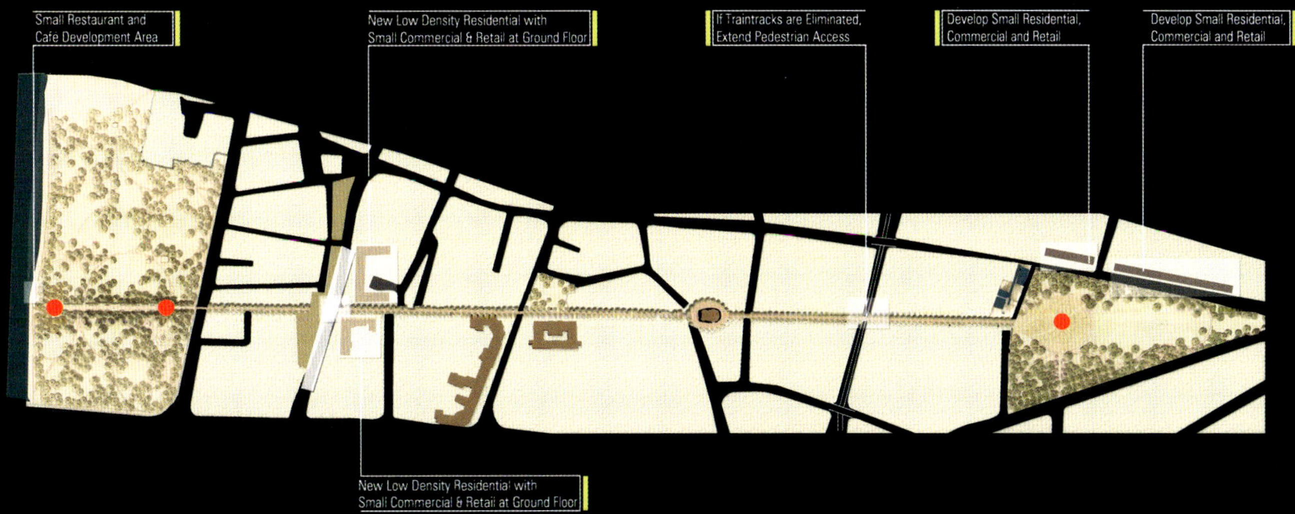

The Legacy of Târgu Jiu

William Tucker

OPPOSITE Detail of *Endless Column*, following restoration

BELOW *View of the studio*, c.1926, showing *Endless Column I*, *Bases* and *Bird in Space*. Studio at 8 impasse Ronsin, Paris. Constantin Brancusi Bequest, 1957. Musée national d'art moderne, Centre Pompidou, Paris

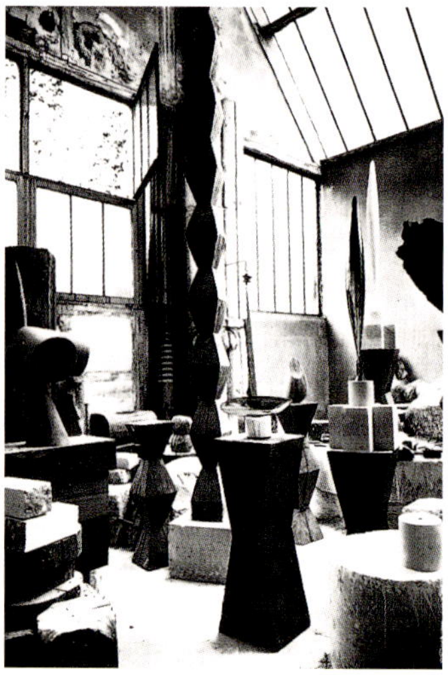

Brancusi warned visitors to his studio not to seek mystery or complexity in his sculpture; they should merely look at it 'until they saw it'. The message was simple: 'I give you pure joy'. The question remained, though, how to communicate this message beyond the Paris studio and the private homes of the (mostly American) collectors of his work. Inspired by the tall buildings of Manhattan on his first visit to America, he began to imagine certain motifs, notably the *Endless Column*, to be executed on a vast scale in the great cities of the modern world, such as New York, Chicago, Paris and Bucharest. In the event, none of these sought-for projects came to fruition, although they were still being discussed almost up until his death in 1957.

In fact, it was an unlikely and unforeseen sequence of events that precipitated Brancusi's only completed venture into public monumental art, in Târgu Jiu. In the course of a few months, between 1937 and 1938, the sculptor created three sculptures that simultaneously represent one monument and yet do not seem to be monuments at all. The ensemble is equally sculpture, architecture and landscape; part of the town, yet separate from it; the individual elements modestly scaled, but the ambition radical and heroic. It was central to Brancusi's thought that the viewer should not be made to feel 'like an atom' (Brancusi) while standing in front of the sculpture.

A more conventionally ambitious monument in a more conspicuous location would scarcely have survived the 50 years of totalitarian rule that engulfed Eastern Europe soon after the completion of the work. Perhaps with a sense of the coming catastrophe, Brancusi left Romania even before the dedication, never to return. Moreover, there is no evidence of any correspondence about the condition of the sculptures in the last 20 years of his life. Thrust into historical time and the conditions of its location, the works at Târgu Jiu have survived and acquired a sense of permanence – of inevitability even – despite the insensitive physical development of the town around them and the hostile political and social climate. They stand in contrast to Brancusi's reconstructed studio in Paris, which feels artificial and frozen in time, like a stage set or a museum diorama.

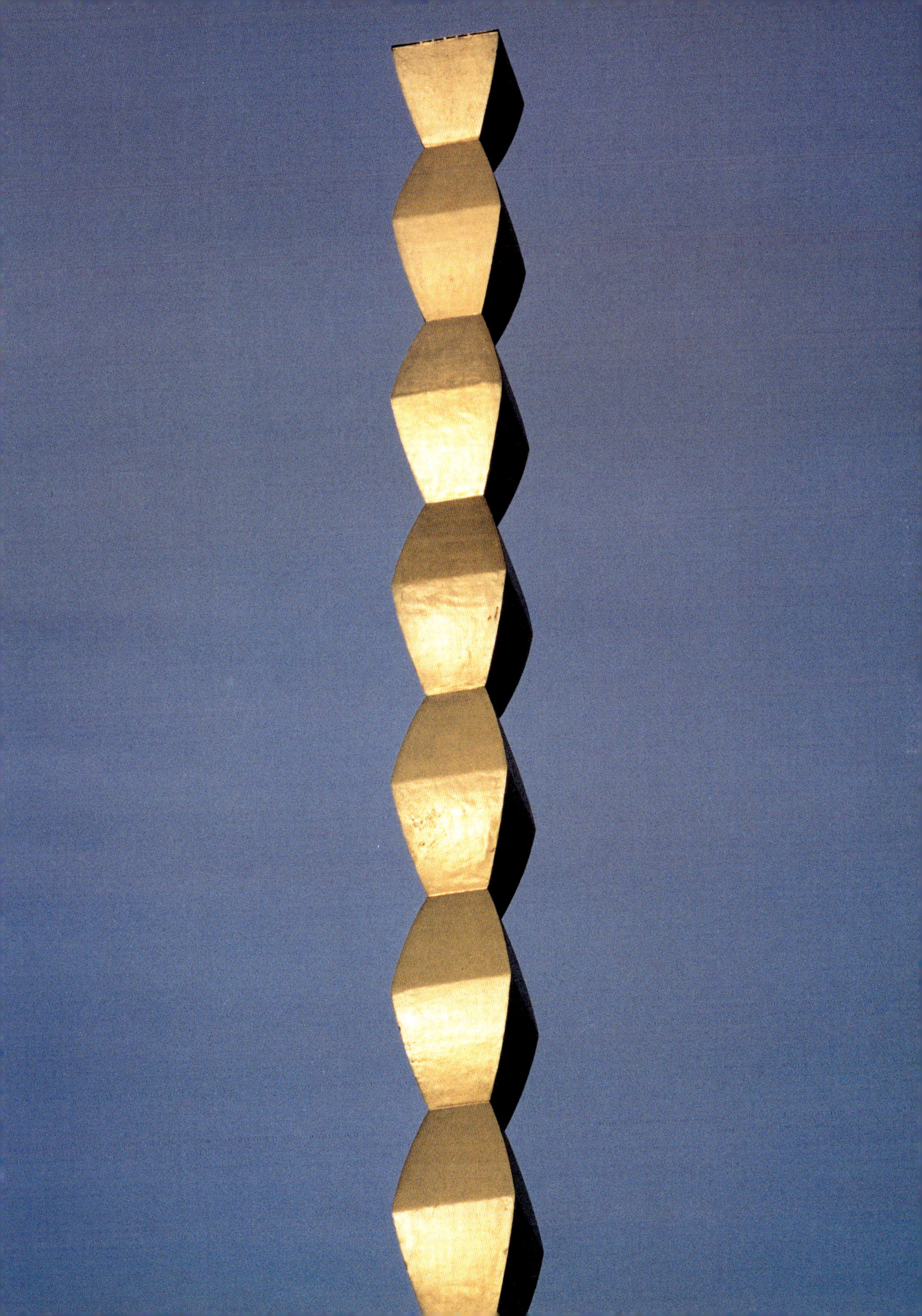

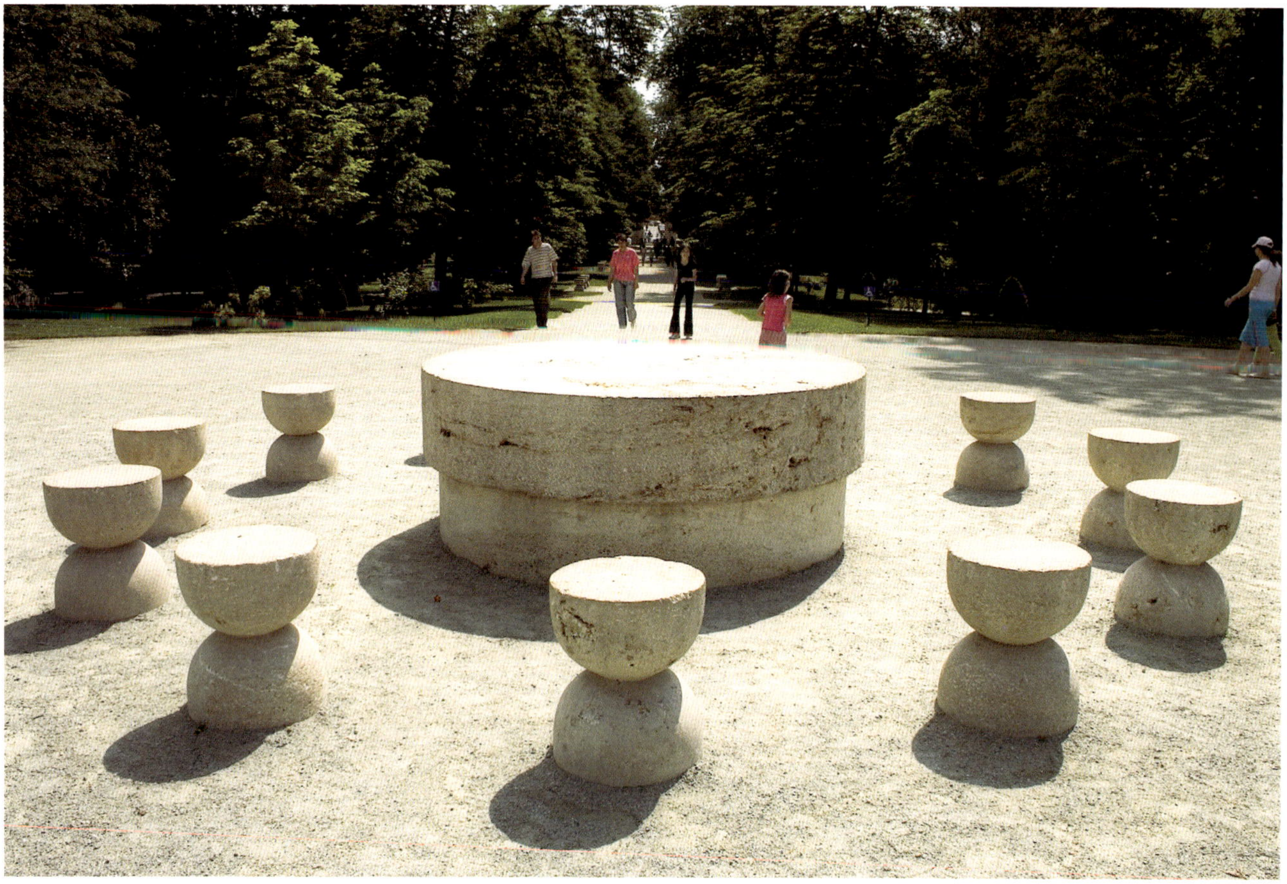

During his lifetime, Brancusi was not only working on new sculpture but re-arranging the elements in his studio, in order to make photographs and to challenge his visitors' perceptions as well as his own. Often in these photographs one can see groupings of objects, whether actual or visual, in relation to the view or distance from the camera, whose composition creates virtual monuments that exist only in the photographic record of the instant the picture was taken. The play of light and shade, and the accidents of foreshortening and overlapping, override the identity of particular sculptures, the distinctions between finished sculptures and those in progress, bases, furniture, moulds, tools and studio bric-a-brac.

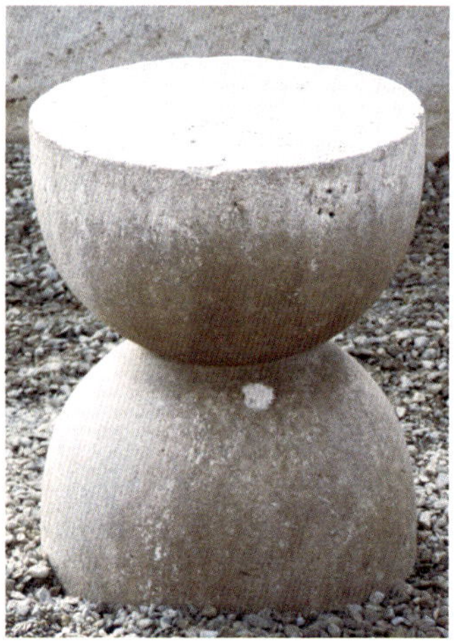

These photographs cause one to reflect on what is constant and what is mutable in Brancusi's sculpture, both on show in galleries and museums, and in the ensemble at Târgu Jiu. In the studio the degree of finish – from the perfection of the marble carvings and the high polish of the bronze castings to the more open treatment of wood and limestone – was carefully controlled by the sculptor. The carved and constructed bases were initially invented to ensure the sculpture was correctly presented after it left his studio. The form of the sculpture is enclosed, its implied movement contained within itself. As opposed to the bases and studio furniture, there are few of Brancusi's sculptures whose top surface is completely flat and level, therefore avoiding the accumulation of dust or the support of another object.

The sculptures at Târgu Jiu all have horizontal upper surfaces; they are

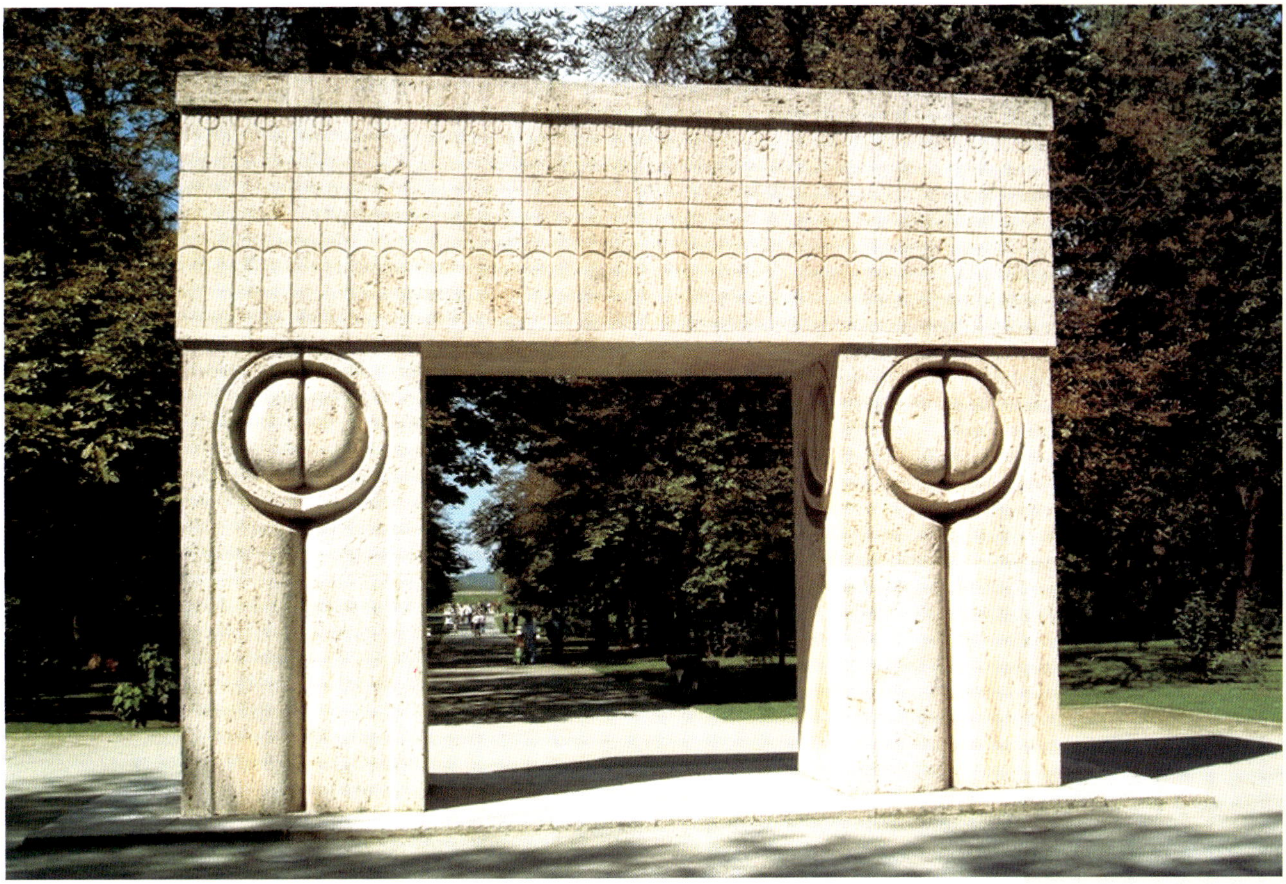

ABOVE The restored *Gate* looking towards the *Table* in the distance

OPPOSITE, TOP *Table of Silence* after restoration, showing the 'horizontal upper surfaces; they are open to the sky and the elements'

OPPOSITE, BELOW One of the stools, after restoration of the stonework

open to the sky and the elements. They are akin to the bases rather than the human and animal motifs of the studio sculpture, lacking the individual, characteristic identities of bird, fish or other animal and human subjects. The *Table of Silence*, *Gate of the Kiss* and *Endless Column* are less-defined propositions. The *Gate*, for example, is both a genuine gate (but not the gate to the park) and an image of a gate. It is also the multiple image of pairs of embracing lovers lightly incised on the lintel and deeply cut into the piers. Yet what it is and what it *represents* seem less significant than what it *does*, how it at once articulates the whole idea of the ensemble and engages, at the deepest and most unspoken level, the responses of the observer, whether resident of the town, casual visitor or conscious tourist. The perfectly judged proportions of inner to outer profiles, between the massiveness of the piers and the lightness of the lintel, and the warmth and texture of the stone, invite and embrace the observer.

On a weekend evening in warm weather the public park is always crowded. Many choose to walk through rather than around the *Gate*, notably children and young couples, who invariably stop and embrace as they pass through. It seems no accident that the *Gate*, in contrast to the *Table* and *Column*, has survived practically intact over the last 70 years, which includes the darkest half century in Romania's history.

Looking west through the *Gate*, down the tree-lined path through the park, one can just make out the horizontal slab of the *Table* against the

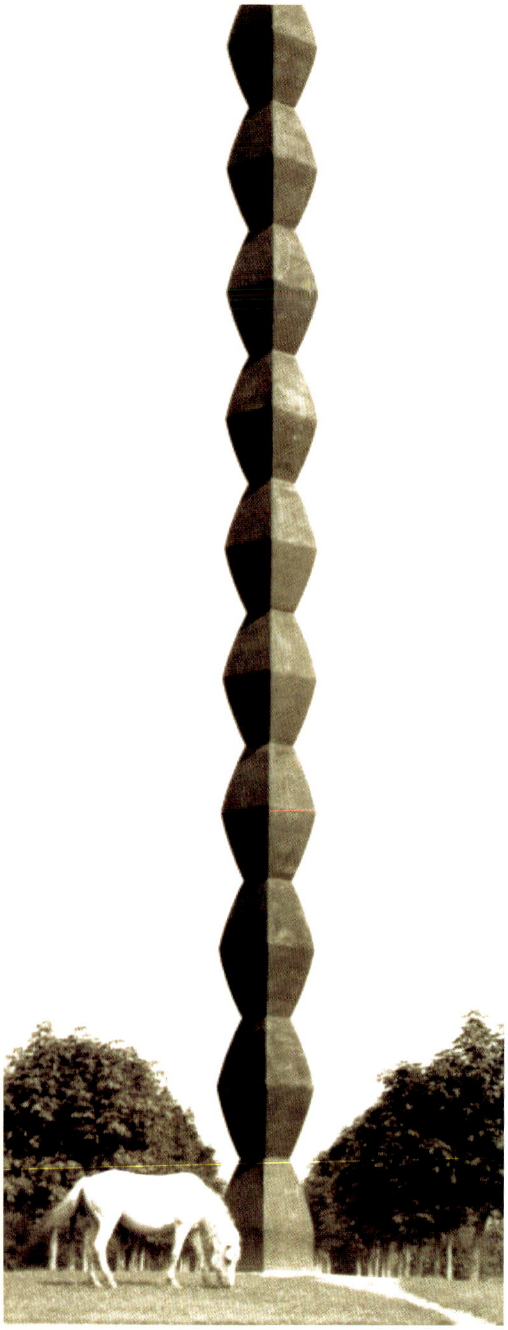

ABOVE *Endless Column*, looking along Avenue of the Heroes, c.1940s

OPPOSITE *Endless Column* at sunrise, silhouetted against the sky

grassed embankment along the river. In the other direction, the arch of the gate frames a distant view of the Church of the Holy Apostles Peter and Paul at the end of a street, itself crossed by other busy streets. The line from the *Table* through the *Gate* continues invisibly down the nave of the church; and standing outside the eastern end of it, one can just distinguish the vertical of the *Column* from the trees and utility poles on the Avenue of the Heroes. Walking down this street in the hour before dawn, the continuous din of barking dogs and cock crows is a reminder of the small market town Târgu Jiu once was 70 years ago. As the eastern sky starts to lighten, one hears sounds of the modern world: diesel trucks warming up and the first trains coming through on the tracks, which have to be crossed before approaching the *Column*. A while later women, either alone or in small groups, enter the park and pass the *Column* with indifference, while en route to the clothing factory, whose grim bulk now diminishes the presence of the extraordinary structure of the *Column* – this 'string of beads' whose under-surfaces are glowing in the first sunlight.

In 1935, when Brancusi's proposal for the Târgu Jiu project was accepted, the site he had chosen for the *Column* was an open field beyond the town. The church, originally built in 1734 and demolished in the 1920s, was being rebuilt. Perhaps it was this that suggested to the sculptor that the church's traditional axis might be extended in each direction, which would, in effect, create an invisible horizontal column that would run from the actual *Column* in the east to the river in the west, and would trace in the landscape the path of the sun and moon across the sky. Trees would be cleared in the wooded Municipal Park to define the axis, and a gate created to frame it. The axis would terminate at the river, whose horizontal flow could be mirrored in the form of the *Table*. But one can equally imagine the *Table* as the base of a vertical column of air, truly infinite in dimension. The circular stools that surround the table and the square stools (or benches) that punctuate the edges of the path, whimsically refer to the motif of the *Endless Column* itself in the negative, the superimposed half-modules signifying compression rather than expansion.

The sense of play and of improvisation in such touches belies the seemingly planned programme of the ensemble at Târgu Jiu. The idea that started as an isolated monument outside the town became, in a series of inspired steps, the articulation of a new kind of sculpture, made from the elements in the existing landscape – the church, the wooded park and the river – as much as the local stone from which the *Table* and *Gate* are carved. Moreover, just as the idea of the sculpture developed and changed in relation to the natural and man-made features of its environment, so it continues to develop in the perception and memory of the onlooker. In the Municipal Park, the sculptures seem at rest and thus completely stable. Everything around is in motion – the foliage changing with the season; cast shadows growing or contracting according to the time of day; people standing, seated, walking or conversing; the light of the declining sun down the broad gravelled path; and the moon setting over the embankment, observed when one is seated at the *Table*.

And the *Column*, in its open field, continually changes as the light changes

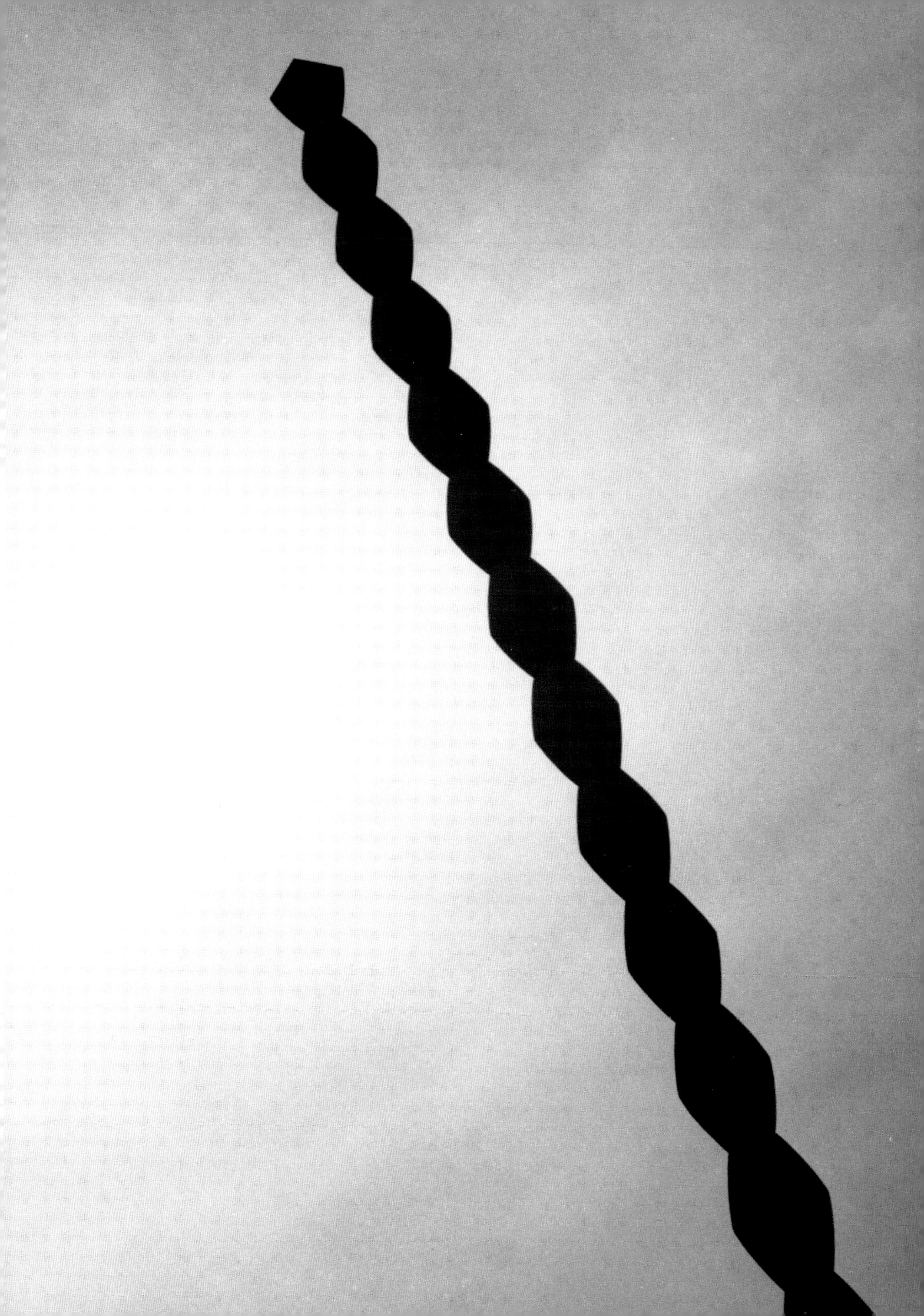

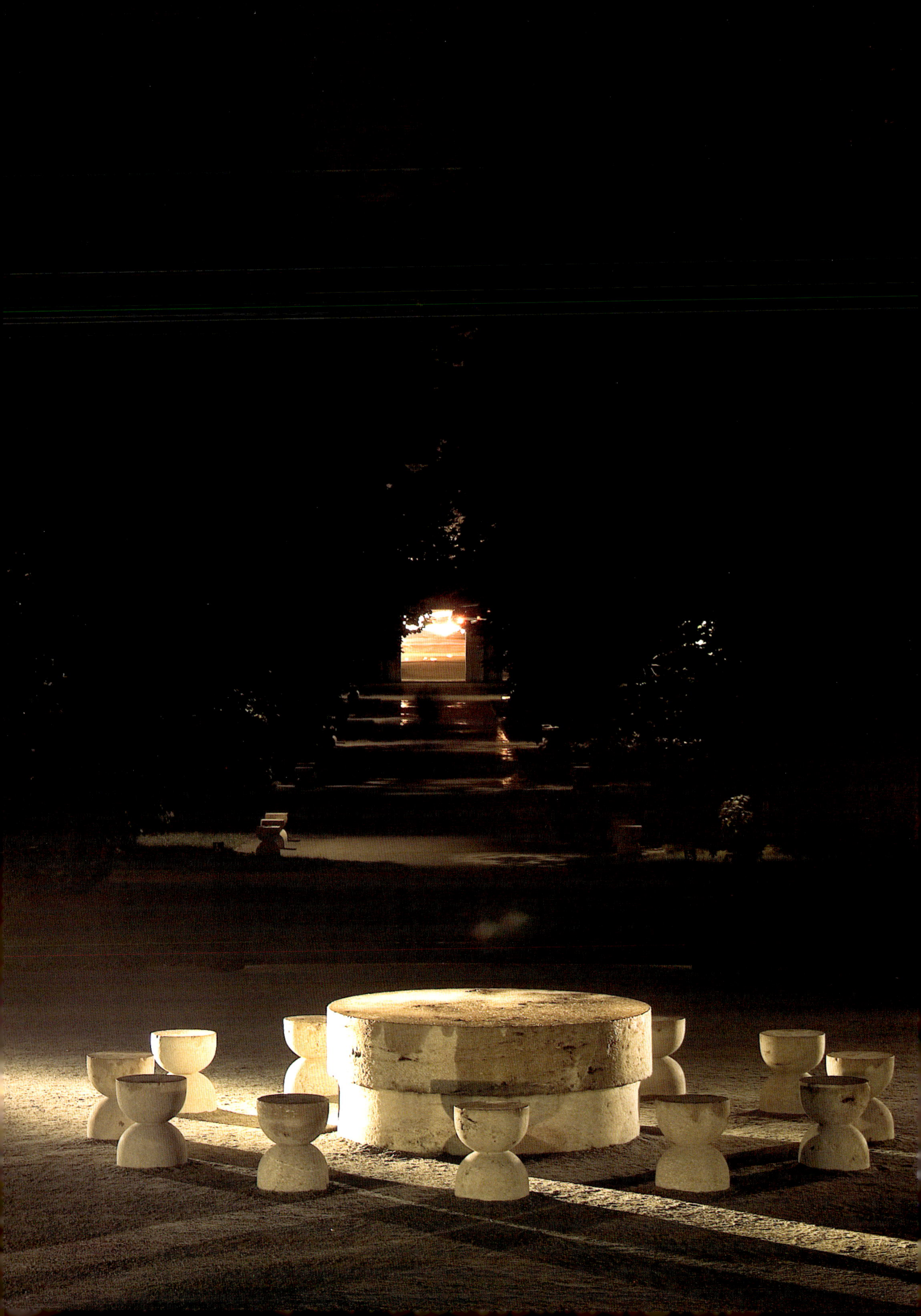

and as the viewer's distance and viewpoint change. All 15 full elements are known to be the same size, cast from the same original wooden pattern; however, seen from any point where the elements can be discerned as separate, no two are identical to the eye. What is known is contradicted by what is seen. Silhouetted dark against the sky, the two profiles take on an independent life; our sense of volumetric against flat, of curved against straight, is continually challenged. Solidly rooted in the ground, the *Column* also seems suspended from above. It exists in relation to the sky and the weather, the light from sun or moon, the ever-varying formation of clouds and now vapour trails. One thing only about the *Column* is constant to the eye: it is not always visible and having only two dimensions – it is a line, an edge. Brancusi set the square plan of the base element on its foundation so that the linear axis of the ensemble, from the centre of the *Table* through the *Gate* and church, runs through the *diagonal* of the *Column*. Visible if one stands on the line from the church, the axis is manifest as the leading edge of each element. Also, under conditions where one side of the sculpture is strongly illuminated, the inner edge of the dark side presents an absolutely plumb vertical of almost 30 metres.

The elements meditated on in Brancusi's Paris studio for years and executed in two successive summers of intense work on site in Romania, enter historical time as they enter the public space. But in their repeated forms they echo the endless cycles of day and night, and the seasons of the year. Their 'subjects' are the immemorial cycles of the human community – the ritual feast; the *Table*, marriage; the *Gate*, death; and the *Endless Column*, which is the garlanded young fir pole still to be seen in the region's rural cemeteries. A fragment from Brancusi's archive reads:

Brad la nunta
Brad la moarte
Dandu [-] ti sama
toati [-] s una
una[-] s toate

Fir tree for wedding
Fir tree for death
As you realize [this]
[you may conclude]
All is one
One is all

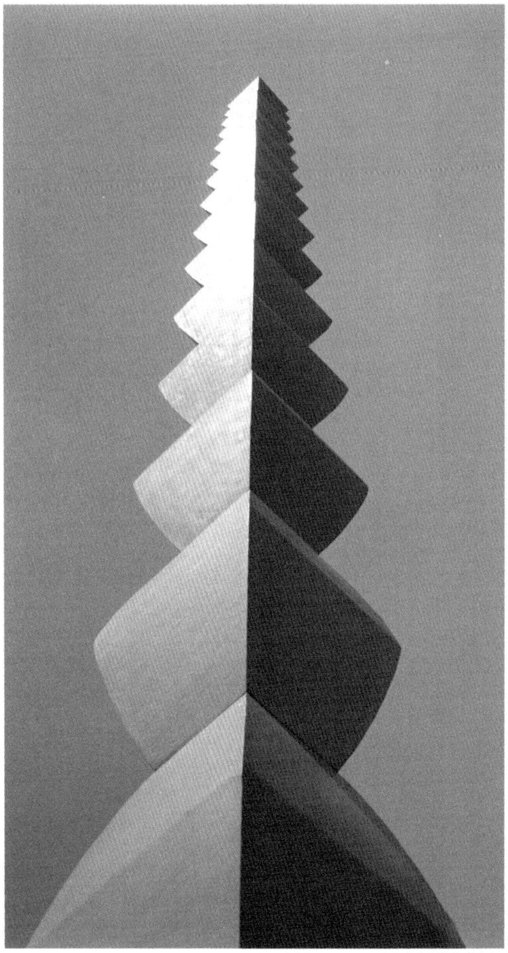

OPPOSITE The new lighting scheme emphasizes the form of the *Table* by using an asymmetric layout of light fittings

ABOVE *Endless Column*, following restoration

Acknowledgements

Since the early 1990s, scores of people have helped in countless ways in the effort to preserve and display Constantin Brancusi's monumental ensemble in Târgu Jiu, Romania. The need to conserve this great sculptural work was brought to the attention of the World Monuments Fund (WMF) when the International Brancusi Foundation (IBF), led by the Romanian artist Radu Varia, successfully nominated the site to WMF's 1996 list of 100 *Most Endangered Sites* with the endorsement of the Romanian Ministry of Culture. At that time, the *Column* had already been disassembled for study by IBF, and this organization then in turn invited WMF to join the restoration project. Shortly after including the site on its inaugural Watch® list, WMF carried out two missions to Romania to assess the condition of the Monumental Ensemble and to develop a means to preserve it. Ultimately, WMF would become the principal partner in the restoration with the Ministry of Culture and Sports. IBF lacked the necessary technical and financial resources to advance the project.

In the spring of 1998, at the instigation of the minister of culture, Ion Caramitru, and his staff, including secretary of state for culture, Maria Berza, and Yvette Fulicea – and with WMF playing a key role in facilitating this arrangement – the World Bank became actively involved in the restoration, agreeing to fund a portion of the work through a Learning and Innovation Loan. This, in turn, led to the formation of a Project Implementation Unit (PIU) within the Ministry of Culture. Thomas Blinkhorn, project manager for the World Bank, spearheaded the effort, supported by Paula Olteanu, director of the PIU. Mariana Moarcas coordinated the World Bank's financing of the restoration within Romania, with the endorsement of James Wolfensohn, then president of the World Bank, and Owaise Saadat, its country manager. The *Endless Column* structure was restored in December 2000 under the supervision of Ion Caramitru. In 2001, Razvan Teodorescu assumed the post as minister of culture, and since then has been instrumental in moving the project forward to completion. WMF is also grateful to secretary of state, Ion Hidegcuti; public works director and secretary of state, Ileana Tureanu; and the director of historic monuments, Dan Nicolae.

The Municipality of Târgu Jiu, Romania, provided logistic and in-kind support, and approvals for all aspects of the project. WMF is grateful to mayor Florin Carciumaru, vice mayor Ioan Roman Barbuti, vice mayor Gabriel Sanda, Marius Ionescu and Paul Popescu, director of the Centrul Cultural, Târgu Jiu.

WMF's project team was led by Mihai Radu, AIA, of Radu Architects. Contractors for the restoration of the Brancusi ensemble included Turbomecanica (*Endless Column* contractor); Plasma Jet (metal plating) and Union of Plastic Artists (technical documents); the Olin Partnership (landscape planning) and Rostrada (landscape architecture); and Consmin Petrosani (landscape contracting). Restoration of the *Gate of the Kiss* and the *Table of Silence* was carried out by Paolo Pagnin. The Romanian branch of Radu Architects supported the project throughout its execution. Special thanks go to Paul Lupu, Oana Crisan, Cameron Sinclair, Petre German and Gina Matsui.

Historians, restoration specialists and consultants within Romania and from around the world guided the completion of the project. WMF would especially like to acknowledge the following individuals for their contributions:

Alexandra Parigoris, University of Leeds, UK
Doina Boariu, Landscape Architect, Rostrada, Bucharest
Ioan Serban Ciorapciu, President, Turbomecanica, Bucharest
David Collens, Storm King Art Center, Mountainville, NY
Mircea Constantinescu, Romanian National History Museum, Bucharest
Mircea Crisan, Engineer, Institute of Architecture 'Ion Mincu', Bucharest
Giorgio Croci, University of Rome 'La Sapienza'
Dorin Danila, Restoration Specialist, Bucharest
Francisc Dosza, Restoration Specialist, Romanian National History Museum, Bucharest
Florin Fagareseanu, Restoration Specialist, Romanian National History Museum, Bucharest
Stephen Kelley, AIA, SE, Wiss, Janney, Elstner Associates, Inc.
Alexandru Lelutiu, Restoration Specialist
Dan Mohanu, National Commission of Historical Monuments, President of the Artistical Components Commission, Romania
Sergiu Nistor, General Director, Department of Cultural Heritage, Ministry of Culture, Romania
Richard Newton, Olin Partnership, Philadelphia, PA
Laurie Olin, Principal, Olin Partnership, Philadelphia, PA
Paolo Pagnin, Venice, Italy
Richard Pieper, Jan Hird Pokorny Associates, New York
Cedric Profitt, DGT Fabrications
Ion Rosu, SC Vulcan SA
Daniel Surdeanu, General Director, SC Vulcan SA
Crisan Popescu, Architect, Rostrada, Bucharest
Cristina Stroe, Architect, Rostrada, Bucharest
Daniel Surdeanu, General Director, SC Vulcan SA
Marielle Tabart, formerly Atelier Brancusi, Centre Pompidou, Paris
Ion Trusca, Plasma Jet, Bucharest
Union of Plastic Artists, Design team
Radu Viehmann, Turbomecanica, Bucharest

Three World Monuments Fund board members provided active guidance, support and stewardship for the *Endless Column* restoration. They include Mica Ertegün, Lois de Ménil and H. Peter Stern. To them deep appreciation is owed.

WMF is grateful also to supporters of this project, who include American Express, the Belgravia Foundation, The Brown Foundation, Inc. of Houston, Gustavo and Patricia Cisneros, Hester Diamond and Ralph Kaminsky, Isabel Eberstadt, the Charles Engelhard Foundation, Ahmet and Mica Ertegün, Selma Ertegün, the Grand Marnier Foundation, Sachiko Imagawa, the International Music and Art Foundation, the Ellsworth Kelly Foundation, the Samuel H. Kress Foundation, the Hon. Ronald S. Lauder, Donald B. and Catherine Marron, Jason McCoy, The Henry Moore Foundation, Dorit Moustsaieff, Lynn Nesbit, Phyllis Myers, Lionel I. Pincus, Arnold S. Scaasi, Maurice Segoura, the Susan Stein Shiva Foundation, H. Peter Stern and the Ralph E. Ogden Foundation, the Trust for Mutual Understanding, the Robert W. Wilson Challenge to Conserve Our Heritage and many others.

WMF staff members who worked on behalf of the project have included Bonnie Burnham, John H. Stubbs, Laurie Beckelman, Kirstin Sechler, Morris Hylton III, Martha Flach, Angela M. H. Schuster and Riccardo Salmona.

Allen Moore Films, Inc. produced a short film on the restoration of the Endless Column Ensemble, with support from WMF.

WMF would also like to thank Sorana Georgescu-Gorjan for archival photographs from the collection of her father, Stefan Georgescu-Gorjan, and Marielle Tabart of the Atelier Brancusi for archival photographs.

Bibliography

Bach, Friedrich Teja, *Constantin Brancusi: Metamorphosen plastischer Form*, Köln: DuMont Literatur und Kunst Verlag, 2004

Balas, Edith, *Brancusi and Romanian Folk Traditions*, Boulder, Colorado: East European Monographs, 1987

Brezianu, Barbu, *Brancusi in Romania*, Bucharest: Editura All, 1999

Chave, Anna C., *Constantin Brancusi: Shifting the Bases of Art*, New Haven, London: Yale University Press, 1993

Sidney, Geist, *Brancusi: A Study of the Sculpture*, New York: Hacker Art Books, 1983

Georgescu-Gorjan, Sorana, *The Wonderful Story of the Endless Column*, Bucharest: The Publishing House of the Romanian Cultural Foundation, 1995

Georgescu-Gorjan, Sorana, *The Story of the Endless Column / Istoria Coloanei Infinite*, Deva: Editura 'Destin', 2001

Georgescu-Gorjan, Stefan, *Am lucrat cu Brancusi* (I've worked with Brancusi), Bucharest: Editura Universalia, 2004

Hulten, Pontus; Dumitresco, Natalia; and Istrati, Alexandre, *Brancusi*, New York, Paris: Abrams, 1987, and Flammarion, 1986

Jianou, Ionel, ed., *Témoignages sur Brancusi*, Paris: Arted, 1967

Klein, Ida, *Constantin Brancusi: Natur, Struktur, Architektur*, Cologne: Verlag der Buchhandlung Walther König, 1995

L'Atelier Brancusi: la Collection, Paris: Centre Pompidou, 1995

Lemny, Doina, and Velescu, Christian-Robert, *Brâncusi inedit: însеminari si corespondenta româneasca*, Bucharest: Humanitas, 2004

Lemny, Doina, *Constantin Brancusi*, Paris: Oxus, 2005

Miller, Sanda, *Constantin Brancusi: A Survey of his Work*, Oxford: Clarendon, 1995

Mocioi, Ion, in *Ansamblul Sculptural de la Târgu Jiu: Documentar*, Târgu Jiu: Comitetul de Cultura si Arta al Judetsului Gorj, 1971

Tabart, Marielle, *Brancusi: l'inventeur de la sculpture moderne*, Paris: Gallimard, 1995

La Colonne sans fin: Les Carnets de l'Atelier Brancusi, Paris: Centre Pompidou, 1998

EXHIBITIONS

Bach, Friedrich Teja; Rowell, Margit; and Temkin, Ann, *Constantin Brancusi, 1876–1957* Philadelphia, PA: Philadelphia Museum of Art, 1995

Giménez, Carmen, and Gale, Matthew, eds., with contributions by Sanda Miller, Alexandra Parigoris and Jon Wood, *Constantin Brancusi: The Essence of Things*, London: Tate, 2004

ARTICLES

Ion Alexandrescu, 'Brancusi la Târgu Jiu' in *Luceafarul* (Bucharest), XIX, no. 7, February 14, 1976

Al-George, Sergiu, 'Brancusi et l'Inde' in *Revue Roumaine de d'Histoire de l'Art*, vol. 18, 1981

Brezianu, Barbu, in 'Pages inédites de la correspondence de Brancusi', *Revue Roumaine d'Histoire de l'Art*, vol. 1, no. 2, 1964

Georgescu-Gorjan, Sorana, 'Istoricul realizării Coloanei fără sfârsit din Târgu-Jiu (1937–1938)'. *Buletinul Comisiei Monumentelor Istorice*, Bucharest, nos. 1–4, 2000, pp. 56–88

Georgescu-Gorjan, Stefan, 'Brancusi et ses Colonnes infinies – Nouvelles contributions', *Revue Roumaine d'Histoire de l'Art*, Série Beaux-Arts, vol. 16, 1979, pp. 89–104

Georgescu-Gorjan, Stefan, 'The Genesis of the Column Without End', *Revue Roumaine d'Histoire de l'Art*, Bucharest, vol. 1, no. 2, 1964

Alexandra Parigoris, 'Brancusi at Târgu Jiu: the Return of the Prodigal Son', *The Burlington Magazine*, CXXVI, no. 971, February, 1984

Photographic Credits

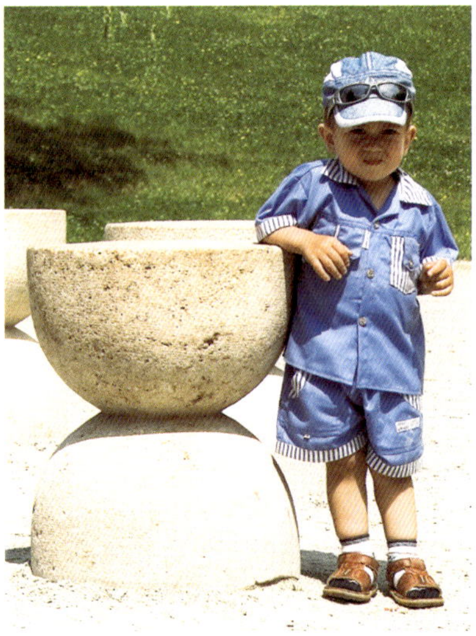

© ADAGP, Paris and DACS, London 2007
Page 13, 15

© Ion Alexandrescu, 2007
Page 25 (top)

© Kale Alford, for World Monuments Fund, 2007
Pages 9, 10, 53, 71

© Dan Calugaru, for World Monuments Fund, 2007
Pages 7, 55, 58 (top), 65, 72, 76

© CNAC / MNAM Dist. RMN 2007. © ADAGP, Paris and DACS, London 2007
Page 14

© Lynn Davis, 2007
Page 77

© Documentation photographique des collections, Musée national d'art moderne, Centre Pompidou, Paris, 2007. © ADAGP, Paris and DACS, London 2007
Pages 21, 26, 40, 70

© Sorana Georgescu-Gorjan Collection, 2007
Pages 31–36, 38, 39

© Giraudon / The Bridgeman Art Library, 2007. © ADAGP, Paris and DACS, London 2007
Page 19

© 2007. Digital image, The Museum of Modern Art, New York, New York / Scala, Florence. © ADAGP, Paris and DACS, London 2007
Pages 18, 20

© Sanda Tatarescu-Negropontes, 2007
Page 23, 24 (bottom)

© Olin Partnership, 2007
Pages 56, 61, 63, 73

© Mihai Oroveanu, Artexpo, 2007
Page 16 (left)

© Mihai Radu, Radu Architects, 2007
Pages 69, 75

© Rostrada, Bucharest, 2007
Pages 57, 58 (bottom), 62

© Tate London, 2007. © ADAGP, Paris and DACS, London 2007
Page 17